FOREVER FREE

MILESTONES IN BLACK AMERICAN HISTORY

FOREVER FREE

FROM THE EMANCIPATION PROCLAMATION TO THE CIVIL RIGHTS BILL OF 1875 (1863–1875)

Christopher E. Henry

CHELSEA HOUSE PUBLISHERS
New York   Philadelphia

FRONTISPIECE   Issued by President Abraham Lincoln in the midst of the Civil War—on January 1, 1863—the Emancipation Proclamation declared that from that day on, all slaves in the rebel states were "forever free."

ON THE COVER   A young Union soldier faces the camera in 1864. At first reluctant to integrate its military forces, the North quickly learned to respect blacks as superb soldiers.

Chelsea House Publishers
Editorial Director   Richard Rennert
Executive Managing Editor   Karyn Gullen Browne
Copy Chief   Robin James
Picture Editor   Adrian G. Allen
Art Director   Robert Mitchell
Manufacturing Director   Gerald Levine
Assistant Art Director   Joan Ferrigno

Milestones in Black American History
Senior Editor   Marian W. Taylor
Series Originator and Adviser   Benjamin I. Cohen
Series Consultants   Clayborne Carson, Darlene Clark Hine

Staff for FOREVER FREE
Editorial Assistant   Sydra Mallery
Designer   John Infantino
Picture Researcher   Ellen Barrett Dudley

First Printing

1 3 5 7 9 8 6 4 2

Library of Congress Cataloging-in-Publication Data

Henry, Christopher E.
   Forever free : from the Emancipation Proclamation to the Civil Rights Bill of 1875, 1863–1875 / Christopher E. Henry.
      p. cm. — (Milestones in Black American history)
   Includes bibliographical references and index.
      ISBN 0-7910-2253-6
      ISBN 0-7910-2679-5 (pbk.)
1.Afro-Americans—History—1863–1877—Juvenile literature. [1. Afro-Americans—History—1863–1877.] I. Title. II. Series.
E185.2.H46 1995
323.1'196073'09034—dc20   94-33636
                                                                                              CIP
                                                                                              AC

CONTENTS

✳

MILESTONES IN BLACK AMERICAN HISTORY

INTRODUCTION

✳

With both the North and the South claiming that they were fighting for freedom, the Civil War had been dividing the Union for one and a half years when President Abraham Lincoln announced to his cabinet on September 22, 1862, that the time had arrived to issue an earthshaking declaration: a proclamation of emancipation. Lincoln informed his close advisers that on January 1, 1863, he would declare that all persons held as slaves in any state still in rebellion against the Union "shall be then, thenceforward, and forever free." The cabinet approved the president's plan, and on New Year's Day, 1863, Lincoln put his signature on the final draft of the Emancipation Proclamation, a document that set into motion an extraordinary epoch in black American history.

The dozen years that followed the enactment of the Emancipation Proclamation saw Americans of color move from bondage to freedom, from political impotence to civil power. These were the years that the thirteenth, fourteenth, and fifteenth amendments to the U.S. Constitution were ratified; respectively, the amendments outlawed slavery, granted citizenship and equal protection of the laws to all persons born or naturalized in the United States, and forbade the denying of a citizen's right to vote "on account of race, color, or previous condition of servitude." Afterward came the passage of the Civil Rights Act of 1875, which prohibited racial discrimination in public accommodations and mandated that blacks be treated equally with whites in regard to jury duty.

At last part of the political process, blacks were allowed in congressional galleries. They were permitted to practice law before the

Supreme Court. They were also admitted to social functions at the White House, with Lincoln taking the time during his second inaugural reception to greet Frederick Douglass, the noted abolitionist. "Here comes my friend Douglass," the president intoned in a voice loud enough for everyone around him to hear.

For the illustrious figures in the fight for emancipation—Douglass, Harriet Tubman, and Sojourner Truth among them—along with the rest of black America, the years that followed the Emancipation Proclamation were filled with stunning contrast. Lighted by soaring hope and dreams of limitless opportunity, they were also shadowed by discrimination, racial violence, and social injustice. In the midst of this era of promise and threat, black men and women began to distinguish themselves in an ever-widening variety of fields. Writer Frances Ellen Harper, inventor Elijah McCoy, physician Rebecca Lee Crumpler, soldier-engineer Henry Ossian Flipper, and lawyer Mary Ann Shadd Cary were just a handful of the African Americans who broke new ground in the years that followed the Civil War. Here is the story of the lives black Americans lived in these years when, for the first time in history, every American could look toward a future of unending freedom.

MILESTONES
1863–1875

✴

1863 • January 1: Abraham Lincoln, the 16th president of the United States, issues the Emancipation Proclamation, technically freeing all slaves in Confederate territory and legalizing the enlistment of former slaves in Union forces.

• March: Congress passes the nation's first draft law, leading to the most violent racial riots in American history. In New York City an estimated 60,000 men, women, and children tear up roads and railroad tracks, burn a black orphanage to the ground, and beat and murder many African Americans.

• July: The all-black 54th Massachusetts Regiment stages a heroic attack on Confederate Fort Wagner, South Carolina, losing 14 of its 22 officers and 255 of its enlisted men. One of many magnificent demonstrations of valor by black Union troops, the attack vastly increases the respect of white northerners for African Americans.

• Mary Ann Shadd Cary becomes the only woman designated as a recruiter for the Union Army. Cary would go on to receive a law degree from Howard University in 1870 , making her America's first female African American lawyer.

1864 • Rebecca Crumpler becomes the first black American woman to earn a formal medical degree.

1865 • April 9: The Civil War ends as Confederate general Robert E. Lee surrenders to Union general Ulysses S. Grant at Appomattox Courthouse, Virginia.

• The ratification of the Thirteenth Amendment to the U.S. Constitution frees all slaves, including those not liberated by the Emancipation Proclamation.

- Congress establishes the Bureau of Freedmen, Refugees and Abandoned Lands—known as the Freedmen's Bureau—in an attempt to supply food, education, and justice to the four million newly emancipated black Americans.

1866 • Black regiments—the 24th and 25th infantries—are authorized by Congress to settle "the Indian problem" in the West. The Plains Indians, in a show of respect for these military men, dub them "Buffalo Soldiers."

1867 • Nathan Bedford Forrest organizes the terrorist group Ku Klux Klan in Nashville, Tennessee, and it rapidly becomes the South's most threatening manifestation of white supremacy. The Klan practices methods of intimidation—including lynchings and firebombing churches—to maintain its goal of keeping blacks "in their place."

1868 • W. E. B. Du Bois, who will become one of black America's leading scholars and activists, is born on February 23.

- The Fourteenth Amendment to the U.S. Constitution—which includes blacks in its definition of U.S. citizenship and guarantees all citizens equal protection under the law—is ratified.

1870 • Due to the ratification of the Fifteenth Amendment to the U.S. Constitution, the denial of any citizen's right to vote "on account of race, color, or previous condition of servitude," is forbidden.

1872 • Elijah McCoy invents the automatic lubricator for railroad engines. This invention becomes so essential that before purchasing a piece of machinery, industrialists begin asking if it is "the real McCoy," an expression still used today to indicate authenticity.

1874 • Blanche K. Bruce and Hiram Revels become the first black men elected to the U.S. Senate. No African American will hold this office again until 1966.

1875 • Booker T. Washington graduates from Hampton Institute. He will return there to teach before starting his own school, the Tuskegee Normal and Industrial Institute, which will become the nation's leading black institution before the end of the century.

• President Ulysses S. Grant signs the Civil Rights Act of 1875, which prohibits discrimination in public accommodations and mandates equal treatment for blacks and whites in regard to jury duty. This bold strike against racial discrimination will be declared unconstitutional in 1877, after the end of Reconstruction and the withdrawal of Union troops from the South.

hood at Montgomery, Alabama, and soon afterward elected Jefferson Davis of Mississippi as its president. By the following June, a total of 11 southern states had seceded from the Union and joined the Confederacy. In May, the self-declared nation established its capital at Richmond, Virginia.

The South's withdrawal from the Union turned violent on April 12, 1861, when Confederate forces began bombarding Fort Sumter, a federal post in Charleston, South Carolina. On April 14, the Union defenders surrendered, a move that brought wild jubilation to the South. Three days after that, Lincoln declared a state of insurrection. The Civil War had begun. The war's roots were twisted and complex: it was fought in part over slavery and in part over states' rights, but it had other roots as well. They were intertwined with economic concerns and the deep differences between the societies of the old, agricultural South and the rapidly expanding and increasingly industrialized North.

Lincoln had long opposed slavery; he called it a "moral wrong and injustice," and said there could be "no moral right in the enslaving of one man by another." As a member of Congress in 1849, he had proposed legislation that would gradually free all slaves held in the nation's capital, and in 1854, he had opposed the Kansas–Nebraska Act, which would have extended slavery into new territories. Nevertheless, Lincoln's principal goal for prosecuting the war against the Confederacy was not the elimination of slavery; it was the restoration of the Union. More than anything else, Lincoln wanted the 11 rebel states back in the young republic.

But first, the president had to cope with fighting and winning the war. Other Confederate victories quickly followed the capture of Fort Sumter: in July 1861, rebel troops routed the Union Army at the first Battle of Bull Run (also known as First Manassas)

As weary Union soldiers (foreground) attend their wounded, the Battle of Bull Run rages on July 21, 1861. The first major engagement of the Civil War, Bull Run was a clearcut triumph for the South.

in Virginia. At this point, Confederate confidence knew no bounds. Bull Run was "one of the decisive battles of the world," crowed a Georgia politician. The *Richmond Whig* declared the war virtually won with the victory, which the newspaper said heralded "the breakdown of the Yankee race."

Battle casualties were relatively low at Bull Run, but as the war progressed, the lists of dead and wounded mounted to horrendous proportions. By the end of the war, the number of Union and Confederate men killed in battle and other war-related causes had exceeded 620,000. No one will ever know exactly how many southern civilians died as a result of the conflict, but one figure is certain: the nation lost more lives in the Civil War than it did in all other wars through the Vietnam conflict (1957–75) combined.

Partly because of these grim statistics, the war was growing increasingly unpopular in the North. In the beginning, northerners had rallied to the cause of maintaining the Union and punishing the South, which, as the Chicago *Journal* put it in 1861, had "outraged the Constitution, set at defiance all law, and trampled under foot that flag which has been the glorious and consecrated symbol of American Liberty." But after the Confederacy's impressive early victories, public and congressional enthusiasm had flagged, and Lincoln knew it would continue to diminish unless he redefined the war. Although not all northerners were passionate about the eradication of slavery, the abolitionist movement enjoyed broad popular support. Representing the war as a crusade to set men free would reinvigorate the North's zeal for defeating the Confederacy, thereby saving the Union—Lincoln's immovable goal.

In midsummer 1862, Lincoln weighed the idea of declaring all the Confederacy's slaves free. As the nation's commander in chief, he had the power to confiscate enemy property, including slaves; he did not, however, have constitutional authority to take the property of citizens who lived in Union states, including slaveholding Maryland, Tennessee, and Missouri. But when Lincoln discussed an emancipation order with his cabinet members in July 1862, they persuaded him to hold off. In light of all the recent Confederate victories, such a move might, as Secretary of State William Seward put it, be seen "as the last measure of an exhausted government, a cry for help."

The following September, Union forces won the important Battle of Antietam, repelling Confederate general Robert E. Lee's invasion of Maryland. Five days after this victory, on September 22, an emboldened Lincoln issued a preliminary emancipation proclamation. Unless the states then in rebellion returned to the Union by January 1, 1863, he said, all slaves within those states' borders would "be then, thenceforward, and forever free." The Confederate states paid no attention, but no one had expected them to. What this declaration did do was turn the Union army into a force for liberation.

"We shout for joy that we live to record this righteous moment. . . .'Free forever' oh! long enslaved millions . . . Suffer on a few days in sorrow, the hour

A Union burial detail performs its grim task on the site of Second Bull Run, the bloody battle waged at Manassas, Virginia, in August 1862. A limited victory for the South, the fight cost both sides thousands of casualties.

of your deliverance draws nigh!" exclaimed Frederick Douglass, the brilliant former slave who had become the nation's leading black abolitionist. His white abolitionist counterpart, William Lloyd Garrison, called the proclamation "an act of immense historic consequence." Union troops and their commanders agreed. "This army will sustain the emancipation proclamation," said one regimental colonel in Indiana, "and enforce it with the bayonet."

Perhaps preparing the nation for the mighty document he would unleash one month later, Lincoln addressed Congress on December 1, 1862. "Fellow citizens, we cannot escape history," he said. "The fiery trial through which we pass will light us down, in honor or dishonor, to the latest generation. . . . In *giving* freedom to the *slave*, we *assure* freedom to the *free*."

As he had promised, on January 1, 1863, Lincoln issued the final version of his Emancipation Proclamation, a document that was to become as much a part of American history as the Declaration of Independence, the Constitution, and the Bill of Rights (the Constitution's first 10 amendments). Lincoln declared that "all the slaves of persons who shall hereafter be engaged in rebellion against the Government of the United States . . . shall be forever free of their servitude, and not again held as slaves." Going further than the preliminary proclamation, this one not only technically freed the South's slaves but legalized their enlistment into the Union army and navy.

The proclamation freed few slaves immediately, but it did swell the Union's military ranks with new

recruits. In New Orleans, for example, General Ben Butler found himself short of men and decided to investigate a local regiment of free black and mixed-race volunteers. He sent for the unit's commander and asked if "Negroes would fight." Respectfully but with confident humor, the black commander shot back,

General, we come of a fighting race. Our fathers were brought
here because they were captured in war, and in hand-to-hand
fights, too. We are willing to fight. Pardon me, General, but the
only cowardly blood we have got in our veins is the white blood.

Eventually, as large parts of the South fell
Union troops, the Emancipation Proclamation

Entitled Reading the Emancipation Proclamation, *this 1864
engraving shows a family of
slaves learning that Lincoln has
declared them free.*

showed its teeth. Before the proclamation, the hundreds of thousands of slaves who rushed to the invading army's side were termed "contrabands," their legal status undefined. After January 1, 1863, slaves in the Union-occupied areas gained instant and genuine freedom.

Throughout the North, people, black and white, waited together in churches, homes, and auditoriums on the night of December 31, 1862. In a black refugee camp in Washington, D.C., an old former slave rose to speak. He said he remembered a time when he had cried all night, because his daughter was to be sold the following day. "Now," he said joyously, "No more dat! No more dat! No more dat! With my hands against my breast, I was gwine to my work, when de overseer used to whip me along. Now, no more dat! No more dat! No more dat! . . . Dey can't sell my wife an' child no more, bless de Lord! No more dat! No more dat! No more dat, now!" The man's speech was interrupted by his friends shouting, "Amen! Amen!" and "Glory! Glory!" At midnight—the hour when the Emancipation Proclamation became official—the entire congregation fell to its knees in fervent prayer.

In Boston, heart of the abolitionist movement, blacks and whites gathered together to wait for confirmation of the proclamation. At the city's Music Hall, an orchestra played Handel's joyful *Messiah* and Beethoven's triumphant Fifth Symphony. When the long-awaited telegram from Washington arrived, people hugged each other, cried, shouted, and pounded their neighbors' backs. "It was," observes historian Page Smith in his 1982 book, *Trial by Fire*, "a strange and moving moment—the blacks, with their expressiveness of voice and gesture, pouring out their hearts; their white friends, far more inhibited in their expressions of triumph, caught up in the exuberance of the moment."

Meanwhile, in the nation's capital, a huge crowd assembled to hear the proclamation. A clergyman on the scene reported that while the document was being read,

> every kind of demonstration was going on. Men squealed, women fainted, dogs barked, white and colored people shook hands, songs were sung, and by this time cannons began to fire at the navy-yard. . . . Great processions of colored and white men marched to and fro and passed in front of the White House and congratulated President Lincoln on his proclamation. [The president appeared on a balcony and saluted the cheering crowd.] It was indeed a time of times. Nothing like it will ever be seen in this life. . . . The first day of January 1863, is destined to form one of the most memorable epochs in the history of the world.

Whatever hesitancy had preceded it, whatever combinations of motives had prompted it, whatever mixed feelings the citizens of the United States may have had before it, the release of the Emancipation Proclamation stirred America as few other events ever have. Perhaps the day's most moving report came from the camp of the 1st South Carolina Volunteers, a regiment of former slaves commanded by Colonel Thomas Wentworth Higgenson of Massachusetts.

To celebrate the great day, hundreds of soldiers, contrabands, and civilians of both races flocked to the South Carolina camp. After Higgenson read the proclamation, the crowd fell silent. Then an old black man began to sing. He was alone at first, but one by one, soldiers and other contrabands joined in, their voices rising in the still night air. The whites started to sing, too, but Higgenson signaled them to silence. "I never saw anything so electric," he wrote later. "It made all other words cheap. It seemed the choked voice of a race at last unloosed."

Clear and strong, the people's song rose into the starry sky:

My country, 'tis of thee,
Sweet land of liberty,
Of thee I sing . . .

2

SERVING THE UNION

IN August 1861, four months after the Civil War
began, abolitionist Frederick Douglass proposed
that the Union army admit black volunteers. "Men in
earnest don't fight with one hand, when they might
fight with two," the former slave told the president of
the United States, "and a man drowning would not
refuse to be saved even by a colored hand."

President Abraham Lincoln might have been expected to accept Douglass's suggestion for a new
source of manpower: at this early stage of the war, the
Union army was reeling, pummeled by the South's
dashing, well-trained cavalry and its superbly trained
commanders. And Washington, D.C., was not only
ill-equipped to defend itself against a major Southern
attack, but filled with Confederate spies and sympa-
thizers. The capital was bordered on the west by
Confederate Virginia; from there, the rebels appeared
poised to overrun the city. Some observers even feared

*An 1860s cartoon shows a white southerner choosing death over
help from a black man. Employing the same image, former slave
Frederick Douglass urged Lincoln to accept blacks in the Union
army: "A man drowning," he said, "would not refuse to be
saved even by a colored hand."*

25

Frederick Douglass, arguably the most influential black man in mid-19th-century America, began life in chains but escaped to become a powerful abolitionist speaker, editor, and writer. Highly respected as he was, however, not even Douglass could change Lincoln's mind about the military enlistment of African Americans.

that a successful rebel attack could result in the capture of Lincoln himself. Assassination rumors swirled through the city, keeping the president's aides in a state of tense vigilance.

Still, at this point Lincoln would not—could not—accept Douglass's proposal. His refusal to accept black volunteers in the army sprang from several roots: one involved implacable opposition from a large proportion of the Union army's white officers and troops, who did not want to serve alongside armed blacks, and who disliked the image of equality that would be produced by wearing the same uniform. Another stemmed from the question of black citizenship, at that point unresolved.

That question had been raised—and for a time, settled—by an infamous 1857 Supreme Court case, *Dred Scott v. John F. A. Sanford*. In that decision, 80-year-old Chief Justice Roger B. Taney, a former Maryland slaveholder, had decreed that blacks had not been citizens at the time of the adoption of the Constitution and had not become citizens since; as noncitizens, blacks were ineligible for military service. The citizenship issue, however, seemed to have little bearing on the recent European immigrants who were enlisting in the Union army; although these men were not yet American citizens, they were white, and therefore eligible for citizenship.

Given that the question of slavery after the war's end was as yet unanswered, some people were surprised that emancipated blacks, known as freedmen, would be willing to fight at all. But thousands of free African Americans showed themselves ready to face any risk, military or political, to end slavery, even without the assurance of universal emancipation by the federal government—which had, after all, sanctioned generations of enslavement. The freedmen may have known little of constitutional law, but they felt confident that the Civil War's outcome would determine their own future as well as that of the Union.

In his autobiography *Up from Slavery*, Booker T. Washington pictures not only the pain and despair of a slave's life but the complexity of master-slave relationships. Powerful in its simplicity, Washington's book describes the typical slave's living quarters: a small, windowless cabin, stifling in summer and freezing in winter, when wind whistled through the chinks in the rough plank walls. Washington remembers slave children eating "very much as dumb animals," being given a scrap of bread or meat at intervals, but at no particular time, during the day. Washington did not know his father's identity; his stepfather, a slave

Georgia slaves line up outside their home in the early 1860s. Housing at least 10 family members, the dilapidated wooden cabin was typical of the accommodations planters provided for their workers.

from a neighboring plantation, visited the family's cabin once a year. When the boy was about six years old his master gave him his first job: shooing flies from the "big house" dinner table with a specially designed whisk.

From that point on, the quality of Washington's life—like that of any other slave—depended on the whim of his master. Some former slaves recalled kind masters and mistresses, but they were probably in the minority. Harriet Tubman, a Maryland bondswoman who escaped in 1849 and later returned to liberate hundreds of other blacks, said that masters "were brought up . . . with the whip in their hand. Now that wasn't the way on all plantations. There were good masters and mistresses, as I've heard tell. But," she added, "I didn't happen to come across any of them."

Northern whites enlisted in the army for a number of reasons: to preserve the Union, to end slavery, or to seek the excitement of life away from farm or village. Black volunteers had different goals. After settling in the North, escaped slaves often looked for ways to assist those they had left behind. Volunteering for military service struck many as the ideal way to help; if there was any moral "high ground" in America's bloodiest war, perhaps it was in the hearts of the freedmen who were willing to give their lives to end slavery.

Some blacks did manage to enlist in the military early in the war. Light-skinned men who could pass for white signed up in substantial numbers, and a smaller group of black recruits enlisted into the more liberal units of the Union army or the various state militias without any objection from white officers. But the bulk of blacks who wanted to fight were kept out of the military. As historians W. Augustus Lowe and Virgil A. Clift point out in their groundbreaking 1984 volume, *Encyclopedia of Black America,* "Ironically, Afro-Americans had to struggle for the right to die in the one war that affected them more dramatically than any other in American history."

The Confederate states admitted emancipated blacks into their military forces as early as 1861, the year the war began, although they were allowed to serve only as laborers. As the war went on, black volunteers performed other services, but none was permitted to bear arms. These blacks offered to help save the nation that had enslaved them for a number of reasons: some felt—as people have felt since the beginning of history—a sense of loyalty toward the land of their birth. Others probably believed that the South would win, and hoped that they would earn a better postwar position by serving in the military.

A Union infantry corporal holds an 1849 Colt pocket revolver in this 1860s tintype (a photograph made on metal). At the start of the war, African Americans met stiff resistance to their military enlistment, but many were determined to serve, and a large number managed to do so.

Still others may have volunteered because they feared being forced into even less appealing activities.

From almost the beginning of the war, the Confederate states debated proposals to draft blacks into active military service. The main argument against it was that armed blacks would surely rise against their masters. By 1863, the debate had grown hotter; in that year, the Alabama legislature voted to enlist blacks in its military units. The following year, Tennessee proposed organizing a division of blacks, promising them freedom at the war's end. This idea, however, was firmly rejected by the Confederacy's president, Jefferson Davis. Even when North and South Carolina,

Georgia, Alabama, and Mississippi strongly recommended enlisting blacks, Davis refused. In late 1864, however, he budged slightly: "Should the alternative ever be presented of subjugation [losing the war to the North] or of the employment of the slave as a soldier," he said, "there seems no reason to doubt what then should be our decision."

In March 1865, the Confederate legislature voted to admit 200,000 slaves into the army. General Robert E. Lee, the general in command of all Confederate armies, supported the move with enthusiasm. Blacks, he said, would make excellent soldiers; they should be enlisted and, at the war's end, freed. Davis finally agreed, insisting only that no more than 25 percent of any area's blacks be drafted. But the move was too late. The South had already effectively lost the war.

The northern military had shifted its policy on blacks earlier. In July 1862, six months before the Emancipation Proclamation took effect, Lincoln's government authorized the enlistment of black men in the Union army. The military recruited blacks not only in the North, but in areas of the Deep South by then under control of Union forces. Because the border states of Delaware, Maryland, Kentucky, and Missouri had remained loyal to the Union, their slaveholders were not affected by the Emancipation Proclamation; these individuals received several hundred dollars for each of their slaves who chose to enlist. The deal was a good one for the slaveholders; two years later, the Thirteenth Amendment would outlaw all servitude in the United States, leaving slave owners with no recompense for their lost "property."

Black infantrymen and their white officer appear on a Union recruitment poster. African Americans time and again proved themselves bold and resourceful soldiers, and by 1862, northern commanders were actively seeking black volunteers.

The Union Army organized black recruits into their own regiments, each commanded by a white officer. Some of these officers were abolitionists who had volunteered for their assignments, considering it an honor to lead black men into battle against the Confederacy. Others were racists; viewing their new commands as demotions, they treated their men with contempt. By the final year of the war, however, black units had achieved such glory that there were more white officers eager to lead them than there were units to command.

Before the war began, about 4 million slaves lived in the South; free blacks in the nation as a whole numbered several hundred thousand. By the end of the war, about 190,000 black men—one-quarter of the able-bodied black male population of fighting age—had enlisted for service. More than half these volunteers came from the Confederate states; they

had gone directly from the rags of slavery to the blue
uniforms of the Union army. They still had to follow
orders, but now they did so proudly, with muskets and
swords instead of axes and shovels. Before the war
ended, more than 38,000 black volunteers in the
Union forces would be killed in action or by other
war-related causes—a higher casualty rate than that
suffered by white recruits.

In March 1863, Congress passed the nation's first
military conscription, or draft law. The legislation
declared all able-bodied white men between the ages
of 20 and 45 eligible for a draft lottery. It also provided
a way to escape military service: a man who received
a draft notice could "purchase" a substitute by paying
the draft board $300. The board would then conscript
someone else; if that person could not produce the fee,
he became a soldier.

On July 3, 1863, the Union and the Confederacy
fought a mighty battle in Gettysburg, Pennsylvania.
The Union won, but—as was the case with most Civil
War "victories"—at frightful cost: 75,000 casualties.
This massive drain on its forces prompted the Union
to put the draft law into effect. Many of those who
could be drafted into the Union army were poor and
uneducated, but they were hardly ignorant of reality.
The war's massive casualties were reported by newspapers and street-corner orators, and those who
missed such reports could see the results of the war
with their own eyes. Trainloads of wounded men
began returning home; civilians grew accustomed to
the sight of veterans, some of them missing arms or
legs, some even begging for their livelihood, on the
streets of New York and other northern cities and
towns.

From the time of its announcement, the draft law
aroused enormous public opposition in the cities of
the North. The idea of conscription was not new to
the world—European armies had been raised this way

Pickett's Charge, a gallant but doomed assault on the main Union position at Gettysburg, virtually ends the decisive July 1863 battle. Costing 75,000 casualties, the bloody encounter forced the Union to pass a draft law, a wildly unpopular move that triggered massive riots in the North.

for centuries—but many Americans saw it as tyrannical and undemocratic. Particularly hostile to the draft law was the governor of New York, Horatio Seymour. Speaking to a huge political gathering of New York City Democrats, Seymour made an incendiary speech: "Remember this," he said, "the bloody, and treasonable, and revolutionary doctrine of public necessity can be proclaimed by a mob as well as a government." To many, it seemed that Seymour was inviting a riot. The audience cheered itself hoarse.

The draft situation was complicated even further by labor issues. During the early years of the Civil War, blacks—penniless, hungry, and eager to perform any work for any amount of money—streamed north by the tens of thousands. Northern industrialists and merchants, who were already making huge profits from the war, saw the influx of blacks as an opportunity to increase their immense wealth. The new arrivals were strong, compliant, and desperate, making them the perfect workers to be used by employers who were trying to gain mastery over a labor union.

In the late spring of 1863, 3,000 New York City longshoremen (dockside cargo handlers) went on strike. Unlike many of today's unionized American workers, these men struggled for survival against primitive labor conditions, ruthless company management, and antilabor courts and legislators. The striking longshoremen, most of whom had immigrated from Ireland, found themselves replaced with blacks who worked under police protection for an even lower wage than the longshoremen had previously been paid.

On the New York docks, labor contracting—along with gambling, prostitution, loan-sharking, extortion, larceny, and murder for hire—was controlled by a handful of gangs. Among them were the River Rats, Dead Rabbits, and Boyos, each numbering a few hundred seasoned fighters. (Tough as they were, the gangs did practice gender equality; some of their most violence-prone leaders were women, including one tavern owner known for biting the ears off any man who crossed her.) Business for these gangs had declined dramatically with the onset of the longshoremen's strike, and their members were ready and eager for action.

With the striking and now unemployed longshoremen, the restless gangs, and the outrage about the draft—made hotter by Governor Seymour's ill-timed speech—the temper of New York City became increasingly unstable as the date of the first draft lottery approached. Underlying all the other resentments lay the simmering anger at blacks. Those men unable to buy their way out of the draft would have to report for service in an all-white army that was committed to freeing black slaves; at the same time, these men had lost their dock jobs to black "scabs"—men hired to break the longshoremen's strike.

A mob cheers after lynching a black man during the draft riots that swept New York City in July 1863. In a four-day orgy of violence, murder, arson, and looting, shrieking rioters hunted down and slaughtered at least 12 African Americans.

The first draft lottery, held on Saturday, July 11, proceeded quietly. But on the next day, the Sunday newspapers printed the names of the men picked by the lottery—1,236 of them—and the rumblings of discontent began to approach a roar. Before sunup on Monday, 500 people, many of them unemployed laborers and most of them drunk, were marching toward the draft office in midtown Manhattan, where work on the second lottery was under way.

When the police learned of the human tide thundering toward the draft office, they tried to turn it back, but they were outnumbered. In such a situation, they might have called in the state militia, but the city's regiments had just marched off to war. When the angry protesters reached the draft office, they broke in, attacked office workers, and destroyed files. Arriving on the scene at this point, a group of volunteer firemen known as the Black Joke Engine Company set fire to the draft office with such skill that it burned to the ground before other firemen could save it.

After that, New York exploded into the worst urban riot in the nation's history, a record that stands to the present day. An eyewitness wrote of the city's First Avenue packed with "thousands of infuriated creatures, yelling, screaming, and swearing in the most frantic manner. . . . The rush and roar grew every moment more terrific. Up came fresh hordes faster and more furious; bare-headed men, with red, swollen faces, brandishing sticks and clubs or carrying heavy poles and beams; and boys, women and children hurrying on and joining with them in this mad chase up the avenue like a company of raging fiends." By this time, much of the city was in the hands of the rioters, who had torn up roads and railroad tracks to prevent federal troops from reaching the beleaguered city. Some 60,000 people, about 1 in every 12 of New York's 800,000 residents, took part in the disturbances.

Much of the mob's fury was directed against blacks. "Down with the bloody nigger!" screamed drunken brawlers. After some hours of general mayhem, 10,000 rioters headed for the Colored Children's Orphan Asylum, a handsome building that stood on Fifth Avenue and 43rd Street (a block from the current

main headquarters of the New York Public Library).
Home to 237 black children, the orphanage resembled
a small version of the White House—a design that
may have sealed its fate with the mob. The matrons
received only a few minutes' warning of the crowd's
attack, but they managed to evacuate the terrified
children and escort them to the safety of the local
police precinct. Just as they left, the mob arrived,
plundered the building, and set it afire. When firemen arrived to battle the blaze, the mob attacked
them and cut their hoses. The orphanage burned to
the ground.

One observer left this report of the scene: "At
nightfall, clouds of smoke hovered over the city
and the stench of burned flesh filled the air. No
longer was one great mob gathered in a single
area; instead scattered gangs spread across the
length and breadth of the city. They attacked any
policeman or soldier who crossed their path, while
lynch mobs openly hunted, tortured, and hanged
every black in sight." No reliable records of the
number of murdered blacks exists, but most sources
estimate the figure to be at least a dozen. Another
hundred deaths, some of them soldiers and police-
men, but most of them rioters, were also confirmed,
and the casualty rate reached at least 1,000. Investi-
gations followed the mayhem, but mob leaders were
never named, and no one was ever indicted for in-
citing the most devastating riot in American
history.

To their credit, most Americans condemned the
riots, especially because of the persecution of blacks.
Recalling the days of terror a week afterward, George
Templeton Strong, a prominent white New Yorker,
called the mistreatment of blacks an "unspeakable
infamy." African Americans, he said, "are among the
most peaceable, sober, and inoffensive of our poor,

and the outrages they have suffered during this last week are . . . inexcusable."

Another first-hand observer, black historian William Pennington, went even further. "An infuriated band of drunken men, women, and children paid special visits to all localities inhabited by the blacks," he wrote, "and murdered all they could lay their hands on, without regard to age or sex. . . . Blacks were chased to the docks, thrown into the river and drowned; while some, after being murdered, were hung to lamp-posts."

Astonishingly, the outrages did not produce un-diluted bitterness in the black population. William Powell, a well-known black doctor, for example, fled his Manhattan home when the bellowing, torch-bearing mob approached. Racing through the streets with his three daughters, one of whom was crippled, Powell was whisked into the house of a Jewish merchant. "Samaritan-like," said Powell afterward, "[he] took my poor helpless daughters under his protection." In the end, Powell—whose son was at that time a physician in the Union army—lost his house and everything he owned to the rampaging mob. This is what he wrote soon afterward: "I am now an old man, stripped of everything. . . . But I thank God that He has yet spared my life, which I am ready to yield in defense of my country."

Civil War infantryman Thomas Waterman Wood reports for duty after losing a leg in the service of his country. Not even such outrages as the draft riots quenched blacks' desire to take part in defeating the slaveholding South.

3

VICTORY OR DEATH

MOST northern freedmen realized—especially after the draft riots—that a Union victory would provide no guarantee of emancipation or of blacks' future civil rights. But because they also realized that a Union victory offered them the only hope of reaching these goals, they continued to enlist in the Union army at a rapid pace. Newly organized black regiments included infantry, artillery, cavalry, and engineering troops. These units were identified not by the insignia USA (United States Army) but by the letters: USCT, for United States Colored Troops.

Predictably, the Confederate reaction to the Union's use of black soldiers was one of outrage. Confederate president Jefferson Davis called the elevation of blacks "the most execrable measure in the history of guilty man," and a soldier from North Carolina described a battle with black Union troops in these words: "Several [were] taken prisoner & after-

The 54th Massachusetts, a celebrated black regiment commanded by Colonel Robert Gould Shaw, attacks Fort Wagner in Charleston, South Carolina, in July 1863. The heroic charge, which claimed the lives of Shaw and 40 percent of his men, finally convinced skeptical white northerners of what one termed "the manhood of the colored race."

BATTLE OF
MILLIKEN'S BEND

A regiment of freedmen, the 9th Louisiana Volunteers of African Descent, attacks rebel troops at Milliken's Bend in Mississippi. Said their white commander after the 1863 battle, "I never more wish to hear the expression, 'the niggers won't fight.' . . . I never saw a braver company of men in my life."

Black soldiers faced danger not only from the Confederacy. When the Union first accepted black volunteers, it segregated them and exposed them to other forms of discrimination, less overt but still troubling. African American regiments were given the lion's share of the army's menial work, such as digging, construction, sanitation, and burial of the dead, a practice that infuriated their commanders, almost all of whom were white. New York's general Daniel Ullman, for example, was in charge of the Corps d'Afrique, an elite Louisiana unit that had performed with astonishing bravery at the successful 1863 Union attack on the Confederate base at the Mississippi River town of Port Hudson.

Leading the charge at Port Hudson was, unusually enough, a black officer. Captain André Callioux, his arm smashed by a Confederate bullet, refused aid and led his men on until he literally fell dead in his tracks. A white officer who saw the charge of the Corps d'Afrique had this to say in a letter to a friend: "You have no idea how my prejudices with regard to negro troops have been dispelled by the battle the other day. The brigade of negroes behaved magnificently. . . . They are far superior in discipline to the white troops and just as brave." After Port Hudson, even the conservative *New York Times* observed that it "settles the question that the negro race can fight."

These were the men General Ullman was told to put to work digging latrines. "The first point to settle is whether it be intended to make these men soldiers or mere laborers," he wrote angrily to Washington officials. "I fear . . . that these men shall be used as diggers and drudges. . . . I have been forced to put into their hands arms most highly unserviceable, and . . . these poor fellows . . . are deeply sensible to this gross injustice."

Perhaps the form of discrimination most troubling to freedmen was inequality of pay. White privates, for example, received $16.50 per month; their black counterparts got $10. The black enlisted men and white officers of one celebrated regiment, the 54th Massachusetts, refused to take any pay at all until the government wiped out the inequality between the races. The 54th marched into battle singing, "Three cheers for Massachusetts and seven dollars a month!" Their wry manner, however, had no effect on their fighting ability; the blazing 54th became one of the most honored American units of all time.

The 3rd South Carolina Volunteers, another black unit of the Union army, responded to the salary inequity problem differently. In February 1864,

William Walker, who had escaped from slavery, enlisted in the regiment, and attained the rank of sergeant through hard work and courage, led his company to the tent of their commanding officer. There, one by one, the men neatly stacked their rifles on the ground. Walker then announced to Lieutenant Colonel Augustus Bennett that he and his soldiers had had a contract with the United States, which they had fulfilled by serving. But the government, said Walker, had withheld their pay, thereby failing to honor its part of the agreement. Therefore, Walker continued, the men felt that their contract with the army was canceled, and they wished to be released from duty and discharged.

Shocked by Walker's unorthodox form of protest, Bennett ordered him to drop the subject and return to duty. Walker refused. He was arrested, court-martialed (given a military trial), and found guilty of mutiny, a capital offense. Walker believed he had behaved in a proper military manner; perhaps the firing squad that ended his life believed the same of itself.

But black volunteer units rarely reacted to salary inequities with insubordination. On the contrary, most tried all the harder to prove their worth as soldiers. Like the 54th Massachusetts, many regiments accepted no compensation, reasoning that to take the reduced salary was to acknowledge inferiority. Some black soldiers went without pay for more than two years before military regulations finally provided for financial equality.

A number of whites also worked to equalize soldiers' pay. In Washington, D.C., influential Republican congressman Thaddeus Stevens did his utmost. "I despise the principle," roared Stevens, "that would make a difference between [white soldiers and black] in the hour of battle and death. . . . The black man knows that when he goes [to the front] that his dangers

are greater than the white man's. He runs not only the risk of being killed in battle, but the certainty if taken prisoner, of being slaughtered."

This reality was not, of course, lost on blacks. The widely read newspaper *Anglo-African* probably spoke for many blacks when it made this statement in a late-1863 editorial:

White Americans remember! that we know that in going to the field we will neither get bounty, or as much wages even as you will receive for the performance of the same duty; —that we are well aware of the fact that if captured we will

Black and white signal corpsmen relax at a base camp. Although most blacks served in "colored" units, a few belonged to integrated companies, none of which reported significant racial friction during the Civil War.

be treated like wild beasts by our enemies; —that the avenue to honor and promotion is closed to us; but for these things we care not. We fight for God, liberty and country, not money. We will fight fearless of capture, as we do not expect quarter so we shall give none. It is infinitely more honorable to die upon the battle field than to be murdered by the barbarians of the South.

The government finally equalized the salaries of blacks and whites in mid-1864: "Having determined to use the negro as a soldier," said Lincoln in a Baltimore speech, "there is no way but to give him all the protection given to any other soldier." Blacks greeted the new policy with delight. To them, it meant far more than the number of greenbacks they got each month; equal pay meant recognition as full members of society. "We did not come to fight for money," said one black soldier, "We came not only to make men out of ourselves, but of our other colored brothers at home."

Another soldier, this one from the proud 54th Massachusetts, described the scene when word of the pay change reached camp: "A pretty carnival prevails," he wrote. "Songs burst out everywhere; dancing is incessant; boisterous shouts are heard. . . . Here a crowd and a preacher; there a crowd and two boxers; yonder, feasting and jubilee." That the 54th could still sing and dance spoke volumes about that regiment. Just a year earlier, in July 1863, the unit had lost not only 40 percent of its men but its young white commander, the popular and highly respected Colonel Robert Gould Shaw. The carnage took place during an appallingly lopsided battle for possession of Fort Wagner, the Confederate bastion guarding the harbor of Charleston, South Carolina.

In the face of murderous cannon and rifle fire, the 54th had charged across a narrow neck of sandy beach toward the fort's heavily defended earthworks. Shaw fell quickly, a rebel bullet in his heart, but his men pressed on, firing their weapons and slashing at the enemy with swords and bayonets. As rebel fire took one black soldier after another, others reached the parapet of Fort Wagner—a seemingly impossible feat—and held it for a full hour. The regiment had been told to expect backup, but when none arrived the unit retreated, 14 of its 22 officers and 255 of its 650 enlisted men dead or wounded.

Later asked about Shaw's body, Confederate officers gave what they thought was a supremely insulting reply: "We have buried him with his niggers." "We can imagine no holier place than that in which he is," responded Shaw's grieving but proud father, "nor wish him better company. . . . What a bodyguard he has!"

The 54th's heroic charge galvanized the North, transforming thousands of former skeptics into strong supporters of the war. "Through the cannon smoke of that dark night [at Fort Wagner]," read a report in the northern magazine *Atlantic Monthly*, "the manhood of the colored race shines before many eyes that would not see." Fort Wagner stood out in the public mind, but it was hardly unique as a demonstration of black fighting zeal. "Hardly a battle was fought to the end of the war," notes historian John Hope Franklin in his 1980 book *From Slavery to Freedom*, "in which some Negro troops did not meet the enemy."

One such skirmish took place at Olustee, Florida, in February 1864. After a particularly fierce struggle between Confederate troops and the 1st North Carolina Colored Volunteers, the white commander of the black unit filed a report. "Our men were brave beyond description," it said in part, "and as their comrades fell around them, they stood up nobly without once shrinking. When the right arm of our color sergeant was broken, he knelt down and held up the dear old flag with his left until relieved."

Less renowned but equally impressive is the story of the approximately 10,000 African Americans who served in the Union navy. Even before the war, the navy had accepted men of all races, but blacks were

THE STEAMER "PLANTER" AND HER CAPTOR.

We publish herewith an engraving of the steamer *Planter*, lately run out of Charleston by her negro crew, and a portrait of her captain, ROBERT SMALLS—both from photographs sent us by our correspondent at Hilton Head. The following, from the *Herald* correspondence, will explain the transaction :

One of the most daring and heroic adventures since the war commenced was undertaken and successfully accomplished by a party of negroes in Charleston on Monday night last. Nine colored men, comprising the pilot, engineers, and crew of the rebel gun-boat *Planter*, took the vessel under their exclusive control, passed the batteries and forts in Charleston harbor, hoisted a white flag, ran

In May 1862, the New York
Herald *ran pictures of Robert Smalls and the* Planter, *a Confederate gunboat the former slave had captured in Charleston harbor. The paper called Smalls's feat "one of the most daring and heroic ventures since the war commenced."*

traditionally allowed to serve only as firemen, coal heavers, mess stewards, or cooks. In spite of that tradition, however, some black sailors managed to take part in the hottest actions. In mid-1861, for example, a group of contrabands—blacks who had been released from slavery by advancing Union troops—signed up on the USS *Minnesota*, where they worked together as a highly effective gun crew.

And in the spring of 1862, a South Carolina slave named Robert Smalls led a band of black dockworkers in the seizing of a Confederate dispatch boat in Charleston harbor. With Smalls in command of the captured vessel, the black crew sailed it under the guns of Castle Pinckney, Fort Moultrie, and Fort Sumter to join the blockading Union navy. The service immediately took Smalls on as a pilot. In another daring exploit, freedman William Tillman, who had been captured aboard a Union ship and declared a slave by the Confederate forces, singlehandedly recaptured the boat and sailed it into New York harbor.

Four black sailors were awarded the Congressional Medal of Honor, established by Congress in 1862 and still the nation's highest military award. One of the medal's early recipients, black gunner John Lawson, served aboard the USS *Hartford*, flagship of Admiral David Farragut. Lawson's extraordinary heroism surfaced during the August 1864 Union attack on Alabama's Mobile Bay, a Confederate naval base guarded by a chain of deadly floating mines, or "torpedoes." (Farragut earned everlasting fame for ordering his fleet straight through this watery minefield. "Damn the torpedoes!" he bellowed. "Full speed ahead!")

As the *Hartford* engaged the enemy, a blast of Confederate grapeshot shattered the right arm of gunner Lawson. Ignoring the pain—and an order to leave

Perched on the rail of his flagship, the USS Hartford, *Admiral David Farragut surveys the battle of Mobile Bay in 1864. After a hands-down victory over the Confederate navy, Farragut recommended John Lawson, a black gunner who had remained at his post despite a shattered right arm, for the Congressional Medal of Honor.*

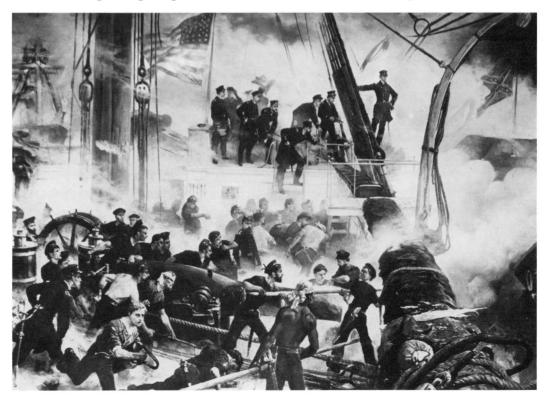

A U.S. warship crew includes a number of black sailors. Some 10,000 African Americans served in the Union navy, which offered them the chance to display their formidable fighting skills and gain the recognition they deserved.

his post—Lawson continued his relentless bombardment of the enemy flotilla. He and his shipmates delivered a smashing Union victory, not only sinking dozens of Confederate ships but capturing one of the enemy's most formidable weapons, the giant ironclad warship CSS *Tennessee.*

Another noteworthy black sailor was Joachim Pease, a crew member of the USS *Kearsage.* All through the war, the Confederate raider CSS *Alabama* had haunted Union operations, sinking and capturing 58 whalers and arms-carrying vessels with a combined value of more than $6.5 million. Finally, in June 1864, the *Kearsage* cornered the Union's elusive nemesis in the waters off the French port of Cherbourg. The crew of the Union ship, which included not only Pease but 14 other black sailors, pounded the *Alabama*, forcing the vessel to strike her colors just before she sank. For his part in the naval triumph, Pease received the coveted Medal of Honor.

> **African American military valor also vastly increased favorable white opinion and treatment of blacks. "It is not too much to say," writes historian Page Smith, "that the entire future of black people in the United States [was] directly and profoundly affected by the performance of black units on various battlefields." As one black Philadelphia woman put it in a wartime letter to a friend, "Public sentiment has undergone a great change in the past month or two, and more especially since the brilliant exploits of the several colored regiments."**

Written in May 1864, the report of a government commission studying the impact of black soldiers included these thoughts:

> The whites have changed, and are still rapidly changing, their opinion of the negro. And the negro, in his new condition as a freedman, is himself, to some extent, a changed being. No one circumstance has tended so much to these results as the display of manhood in negro soldiers. Though there are higher qualities than strength and physical courage, yet, in our present state of civilization, there are no qualities which command from the masses more respect.

By the end of the war, almost 10 percent of the Union army forces had been black: 178,985 enlisted men and 7,122 officers, fighting in 449 battles. The navy boasted 29,000 black men—one-quarter of its enrollment. Along with the four black sailors who won the Congressional Medal of Honor were 17 black soldiers.

4

THE PRICE OF FREEDOM

✦

AS the Union armies rolled over the South, newly liberated blacks reacted in a variety of ways. For those who quickly grasped what had happened, pure joy often prevailed. A young woman from Richmond, Virginia, later gave a moving account of the day she learned of the South's defeat. "I jump up an' scream, 'Glory, glory, hallelujah to Jesus! I'se free! I'se free!'" she recalled saying. Then, she added, "I got sort of scared, afeared somebody might hear me, an' I takes another good look, an' fall on the ground, and roll over, and kiss the ground for the Lord's sake. . . . The soul buyers can never take my two chillun from me; no, never take 'em from me no more."

In some cases, however, the Yankees' arrival proved a mixed blessing to blacks, especially between battles, when land often changed hands from North to South and back again. A former Arkansas slave remembered the soldiers who had ransacked his own-

A black regiment gets a joyous reception at the close of the war. For many enslaved blacks, the arrival of Union troops made the Emancipation Proclamation a reality.

55

ers' "Big House," killed all the livestock, then sent "Old Miss" (the plantation's owner) to the kitchen to cook. His mother, reported the black man, "got scared, and went to bed. Directly the [Union officer] come on down there and said, 'Auntie, get up from there. . . . You can do as you please now. You're free.'" But when the Yankees departed, he recalled with a shudder, the Confederate troops returned.

"One night there'd be a gang of Secesh [southerners; short for secessionists]," recalled the former slave, "and the next one, there'd come along a gang of Yankees. Pa was 'fraid of both of 'em. Secesh said they'd kill him if he left his white folks. Yankees said they'd kill him if he didn't leave 'em. He would hide out in the cotton patch and keep we children out there with him."

Inevitably, a certain number of liberated slaves turned on their former masters. In one case, two young black women approached a Union camp near Jamestown, Virginia, and told black sergeant George Hatton and his men how to find the home and hidden wealth of their master, a Mr. Clayton. The women then displayed their backs, both deeply scarred from savage whippings by Clayton. The sergeant sent his men to the slaveholder's home; they returned with the booty—and Clayton himself.

Hatton ordered Clayton tied to a tree, then handed each woman a whip. They took turns returning Clayton's treatment, reminding him between each stroke, Hatton later reported, "that they were no longer his, but safely housed in Abraham's bosom, and under the protection of the Star-Spangled Banner, and guarded by their own patriotic, though once down-trodden race." Clearly relishing this tale of simple justice, Hatton finished his account lyrically: "The day is clear . . . and the birds are singing sweet, melodious songs, while poor Mr. C. is crying to his servants for mercy."

Thousands of blacks left their homes and attached themselves to the Union armies—in some cases, creating a problem for the liberators, who lacked the facilities to feed and care for these huge crowds. A Union general crossing Louisiana in 1862 reported his situation in these words:

> You can form no idea . . . of the appearance of my brigade as it marched down the bayou. . . . Every soldier had a negro marching in the flanks. . . . Plantation carts, filled with negro women and children, with their effects; and of course compelled to pillage [steal] for subsistence, as I have no rations to issue them. I have a great many more negroes in my camp now than I have whites.

"There are not 50 negroes in the South," added an observer, "who would not risk their lives for freedom. The man who affirms that they are contented and happy, and do not desire to escape, is either a falsifier or a fool."

Hundreds of contrabands—slaves who escaped into Union custody—head for a federal army camp in 1862. One of the nation's most popular spirituals, "Many Thousands Gone," refers to these massive migrations of people in search of a new life.

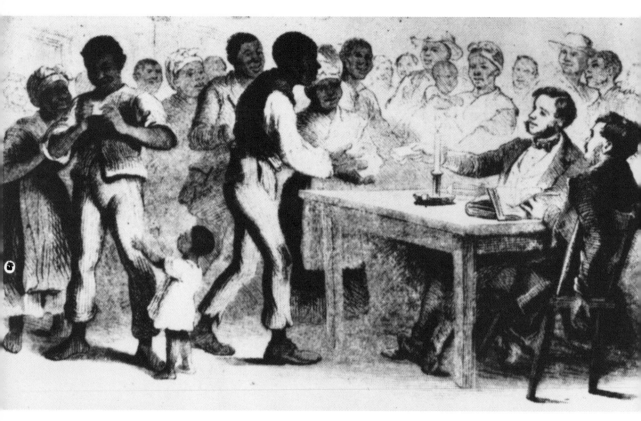

Free plantation workers collect their wages for the first time. Such scenes were more the exception than the rule: certain that their former slaves could not retaliate, many former planters signed them up, then refused to pay them.

Although usually in need of food, the former slaves seemed even hungrier for freedom's most eagerly awaited reward: education. A Union army chaplain in Louisiana had this to say in 1863:

> Go out in any direction and you meet negroes on horses, negroes on mules. . . negroes in uniform, negroes in rags, . . . negroes living in tents, . . . negroes living on the bare ground with the sky for their covering; all hopeful, almost all cheerful, everyone pleading to be taught, willing to do anything for learning. . . . Their cry is for "Books! Books!" and "when will school begin?" Negro women come and offer to cook and wash for us, if we will only teach them to read the Bible.

Blacks could go where they chose after the Union victory, but for some, especially the elderly, a new life as a free man or woman in the North was unimaginable. Many remained with their former masters, who were often allowed to keep operating their plantations if they took an oath of allegiance to the United States. Younger people, too, sometimes remained on their old plantations, believing them the safest places in a world turned suddenly upside-down. Discussing the North's views of the subject, historian Page Smith observes,

> The hope had been that the Emancipation Proclamation would inspire the southern slaves not necessarily to rise in rebellion but to desert their masters and mistresses in large numbers and to refuse to work any longer on their plantations. In this respect the proclamation proved a disappointment. The great majority of slaves remained on the plantations and farms where most of them had grown up, and carried on their accustomed tasks.

New arrangements between former slaves and masters differed chiefly in titles. Slaves became farm laborers or tenant farmers or sharecroppers; masters were now employers or landlords. All their lives, southern blacks had been trained to be subservient and dependent on their masters for everything from food, clothing, and medicine to marriage and job assignments. Ceaselessly taught that the white man was superior, they knew for a fact that whites held great power, they themselves none. Almost no slaves had been taught to read or write, and few possessed marketable skills—aside from farming—or knew anything about the world outside their immediate environment.

In their new circumstances, the South's black people continued to be oppressed, although in more subtle ways. Now they worked for pay, but they rarely received as much as white workers doing the same jobs, and they often had trouble collecting their wages. The occupying Union forces set up rules to protect black farm workers, but planters usually ignored them. Those taking advantage of black farm laborers were by no means all southerners. Northern entrepreneurs began moving south, leasing huge plantations, and hiring black workers, to whom they proved no better employers than their slaveholding predecessors. Smith quotes the report of a government inspector who visited one such leased plantation:

> The poor negroes are everywhere greatly depressed at their condition. They all testify that if they were only paid their little wages as they earn them, so that they could purchase clothing, and were furnished with the provisions promised, they could stand it; but to work and get poorly paid, poorly fed, and not doctored when sick, is more than they can endure.

Most emancipated slaves who ventured forth to claim their freedom owned nothing more than a change of clothing, a satchel of food, a few household items, and perhaps a small number of coins. Many traveled from place to place in search of work or sustenance, although in the years that immediately followed the Civil War, the crushed former Confederacy promised little to whites, let alone blacks.

In the spring of 1865, just before the end of the war, Congress made a massive effort to deal with these four million suddenly emancipated men and women; it established a new department, the Bureau of Freedmen, Refugees and Abandoned Lands, universally known as the Freedmen's Bureau. Under the leadership of General Oliver Otis Howard, a highly decorated Union officer who had lost an arm and won a Congressional Medal of Honor at the Battle of Fair Oaks (Virginia), the bureau faced a monumental task. Its mission: to accommodate the physical, educational, and psychological requirements of all southerners, white and black alike. Most reports credit the bureau with a surprising share of success.

"During its short life (1865–72)," writes historian Lerone Bennett, Jr., in his 1984 book, *Before the Mayflower: A History of the Negro in America*, "the Freedmen's Bureau was . . . an early NAACP [National Association for the Advancement of Colored People]." The bureau, Bennett continued,

stood between the freedman and the wrath of his ex-master. It gave direct aid to some one million freedmen, established hospitals and distributed over 21 million rations [of food], many of them to poverty-stricken whites. The bureau also established day schools, night schools, and industrial schools. Practically all the major Negro colleges (Howard, Fisk, and Morehouse) were founded or received substantial financial aid from the bureau. Handicapped by inadequate appropriations, a poorly trained staff, and the bitter hostility

Symbolizing the Freedmen's Bureau, a soldier keeps southern whites from accosting newly free blacks. Although it was hobbled by lack of funds and southern hostility, the bureau accomplished much in its seven-year existence, feeding the hungry, building hospitals for the poor, and establishing schools and colleges for African Americans.

Students throng the courtyard of Howard University, founded in 1867 by Freedmen's Bureau commissioner Oliver O. Howard. Starting with two academic departments, four students, and one teacher, Howard grew quickly, eventually becoming the nation's premier black college.

of white southerners, the bureau did not do all it could have done. What it did, however, was absolutely indispensible to four million freedmen who were protected neither by law, love, nor greed.

Working with the Freedmen's Bureau or independently were thousands of teachers. White and black, most of them women, all of them almost fanatically dedicated to schooling the nation's former slaves, these educators poured into the South after the war. Adding to their ranks were many who were already there, black southern women who had managed to acquire an education and who were eager to share it with their black sisters and brothers; and white southerners who had for decades yearned to break their society's laws against educating blacks.

The missionary zeal for teaching seemed strongest in the North, where hundreds of organizations mobilized education drives on behalf of the freed slaves. The African Methodist Church, for example, called on "all of our people . . . to give to this cause, for we believe it to be a Christian duty. . . . Let us provide clothing and money to help take care of [the former slaves]; let us send them kind teachers both colored and white." Another northern appeal, this one from a leader in the Israel Bethel Church, said, "every man of us now, who has a speck of grace or a bit of sympathy, for the race that we are inseparably identified with, is called up . . . to extend a hand of mercy to *bone of our bone and flesh of our flesh.*"

Northern whites were both more prosperous and more numerous than northern blacks, and the majority of the teachers who headed south were white. This disparity spurred a Baltimore Methodist clergyman, the Reverend James Lynch, to tell his flock that

Former slave children listen to their teacher in Richmond, Virginia. Touched by the plight of educationally neglected black children, thousands of teachers went south to open schools, most of them under the auspices of the Freedmen's Bureau.

although "the white people are doing in the South an educational work that shines forth as the greatest achievement of this world's six thousand years, [I cannot watch] the entire work of education of thousands of our black brethren being carried on entirely by the whites without appealing to my colored friends to be up and doing." Such calls to action sparked an outpouring of volunteers and money from the black community. "That northern blacks responded as they did out of the pitifully little that they had," observes Page Smith, "is striking testimony to their feeling of solidarity."

In the midst of postwar shock, confusion, and hardship, then, the South's people of color found some reasons for hope and faith in the future. But those rays of light must sometimes have seemed pale and weak, for a dark and monstrous presence loomed over the black South's days and nights. This was the specter of the defeated white South, bitter at the loss of its safe and superior world, hagridden by fear that its onetime vassals would gain possession of the whip hand. For whites, the post–Civil War South seethed with rumors of uprisings and massacres of whites by former slaves. Almost universally baseless, the rumors nevertheless struck further terror into some southern whites, who responded by forming secret organizations to "keep the nigger down." The dark times spawned dozens—including the innocent-sounding Baseball Club of the First Baptist Church, Mother's Little Helpers, Knights of the White Camellia, Red Shirts, and the Council of Safety—but the best known was the Ku Klux Klan, organized in 1867 in Nashville, Tennessee.

Headed by Nathan Bedford Forrest (the "hero" who had led the Fort Pillow Massacre), the Ku Klux Klan concerned itself with keeping

blacks from political power. "How?" asks Lerone Bennett, Jr. "By stealth and murder," he answers, "by economic intimidation and political assassinations, by whippings and maimings, cuttings and shootings, by the knife, by the rope, by the whip. By the political use of terror, by the braining of the baby in its mother's arms, the slaying of the husband at his wife's feet, the raping of the wife before her husband's eyes. By *Fear*."

The Klan defined itself as "an institution of Chivalry, Humanity, Mercy, and Patriotism." A newspaper published by an Alabama "Klavern" (a local Klan chapter) defined the organization and its aims more plainly: "We must kill or drive away leading Negroes and only let the humble and submissive remain." Historians estimate that during one three-year period in the Klan's heyday, its "Knights" murdered at least 20,000 black men, women, and children. This figure

Ku Klux Klan members gather straw for a project, probably the torching of a black person's home. Established two years after the war, the Klan aimed at reducing blacks to political impotence by, as historian Lerone Bennett puts it, "stealth and murder, by . . . the knife, by the rope, by the whip."

does not include an uncountable number of flog-
gings, mutilations, rapes, acts of arson, and van-
dalism.

Southern blacks fought back as well as they could.
Mostly poor, unarmed by law, their means of counter-
attack were limited, but they made good use of the
tools available. "Turn on your persecutors," urged
Faith Lichen, a black leader of the late 1860s. "I know
that you are without weapons," he continued, "but
there is always one by you—the torch. It is fearful, use
it, hurl it with all your might into the mansions of
the wealthy instigator." When they could, terrified
blacks followed Lichen's advice, but they often paid a
heavy price for their daring. A Klan document from
Charleston, South Carolina, contained this statement: "Resolved, That in all cases of incendiarism ten
of the leading colored people and two white sympa-
thizers shall be executed in that vicinity."

Because counterattacks on the Klan were filled
with such extreme danger, blacks relied mostly on
self-defense. All over the South, when a black community received word of an approaching Klan attack,
the people armed themselves with whatever they
could find, then gathered at the schoolhouse, church,
home, store, or whatever other target the Klan had
selected. More often than not, the Klan's white-robed,
masked "night riders" skulked off rather than engage
in an open fight. Still, the score never approached a
tie; the Klan and its murderous imitators continued to
lynch, beat, and burn for decades.

The Emancipation Proclamation technically
freed all slaves in the Confederate states—"technically" because the order of President Abraham
Lincoln had no force in the states in rebellion.

With the South's surrender in 1865, however, all slaves in the old Confederacy were automatically free. The rest of America's enslaved blacks gained their liberty with passage of the Constitution's Thirteenth Amendment, ratified in 1865, soon after the war's close.

Three years later, in 1868, the states ratified the Fourteenth Amendment, which specifically defines U.S. citizenship and guarantees all citizens equal protection of the law. The last of the three so-called Civil War amendments, the Fifteenth, would gain ratification in 1870. Intended to guarantee the vote to the newly emancipated black population, this amendment forbade the federal or state governments to deny or abridge any citizen's right to vote "on account of race, color, or previous condition of servitude." Over the years, the South would try—often successfully—to counter the Fifteenth Amendment; not, in fact, for almost a century, with passage of the Civil Rights Act of 1965, would the southern black be guaranteed safe access to the ballot box.

5

RECONSTRUCTION

W HEN the white South looked toward its future, it beheld a world without slaves—but with a huge population of newly free blacks. Perceiving that population as a massive threat, states, counties, and cities began to pass "Black Codes," laws designed to keep African Americans as helpless as they had been before the war. The majority of white southerners regarded these codes as necessary to their survival for two reasons: first, they assumed blacks to be bent—perhaps justifiably—on taking revenge for centuries of oppression; second, they hoped to restore at least part of their past wealth and power, and for this they needed a labor force of subservient, powerless blacks.

Applying to all blacks, including those whose families had been free for generations before the Civil War, the Black Codes were often more repressive than the laws that had governed slaves. The primary

Blacks run for their lives as white gunmen hunt them down in Memphis, Tennessee, in May 1866. The Memphis Riot was unusually bloody—46 blacks died, 80 suffered wounds, and 12 black schools were set afire—but it reflected the South's mood during Reconstruction, a time when whites saw blacks gaining the upper hand.

purpose of the codes was to limit blacks' personal freedom, restricting them to a type of servitude not unlike slavery. Basically, in the words of historian Page Smith, what the codes did was "deny blacks the most basic political, social, economic, and constitutional rights." In some ways even more onerous than slavery, life under the Black Codes offered none of the advantages—food, clothing, shelter, medical care—that slavery, horrendous though it was, provided its subjects.

The Black Codes specified almost every detail of southern African Americans' lives. The codes enforced in the small Louisiana community of Opelousas were typical:

> No negro or freedman shall be allowed to come within the limits of the town of Opelousas without special permission from his employers. . . . Whoever shall violate this provision shall suffer imprisonment and two days' work on the public streets, or pay a fine of five dollars. . . . No negro or freedman shall reside within the limits of the town . . . who is not in the regular service of some white person or former owner. . . . No public meetings or congregations of negroes or freedmen shall be allowed within the limits of the town. . . . No negro or freedman shall be permitted to preach, exhort, or otherwise declaim to congregations of colored people without a special permission from the mayor or president of the board of police. . . . No freedman . . . shall sell, barter, or exchange any merchandise within the limits of Opelousas without permission in writing from his employer.

Most Black Codes were astonishingly complex, covering every aspect of existence. They specified types of employment permitted: one set of codes ordered that each black person "is to be in the service of some white person or former owner." The South Carolina code dictated that no person of color "shall pursue the practice, art, trade or business of an artisan, mechanic, or shopkeeper, or any other trade or employment besides that of husbandry [farming], or that of a servant under contract for labor, unless he shall have obtained a license from the judge of the district court."

The South Carolina code—typical of those passed by the other former Confederate states—went on to say that if a black laborer quit or was dismissed, he was obliged to "forfeit his wages for that year up to the time of quitting." If a black contract laborer was absent from work, he lost his pay for the days he was out, but if his employer suspected that he was only pretending to be sick "for the purpose of idleness," he would be fined double the amount of those days' pay. Under the Black Codes, an unemployed black man could be treated as a criminal, and sentenced to work without pay.

The codes outlawed marriage or sexual contact between blacks and whites, and specified how blacks should "behave" in the presence of whites. The laws imposed curfews, restricted free speech, kept blacks off juries, and sometimes prohibited them from testifying against white persons, even when they had been personally victimized.

In Alabama, blacks who attended meetings after work for political or other purposes could be fined $50—at least three months' wages—and, if they could not meet the fine, be sentenced to work without pay for a period "not exceeding six months." At the same time, a black man or woman who could not show a "visible means of support"—that is, a paying job—could be "immediately arrested by any sheriff or constable" and "hired out [to] the highest bidder, for the remainder of the year."

Stalked by the Klan and other terrorist groups, many freedmen would have chosen to be armed, but this possibility was cut off by the Black Codes. In most of the South, "no negro, mulatto, or person of color" could possess "any bowie-knife, dirk, sword, firearms, or ammunition." In Florida, a black found with such a weapon could be "whipped with 39 lashes on the bare back."

The ferocity of the South's Black Codes, of course, hardly went unnoticed in the North. Reports of the injustice and cruelty being heaped on freedmen— the very people for whom, in large part, northerners had fought the recent bloody conflict—horrified both blacks and whites. Northerners, particularly Republicans, were also outraged by the public officials elected by the defeated South.

Until their states had rewritten their constitutions, southern senators and congressmen could neither take the oath of office nor vote. Their presence, however, was enough to indicate that the South repented nothing: among the southern delegation were 58 members of the Confederate Congress, 6 cabinet officers of Confederate president Jefferson Davis, 4 generals and 5 colonels in the Confederate army, and the vice-president of the Confederacy itself. (That the South failed to send Davis to Washington was probably due only to his postwar status: he was a federal prisoner in Fortress Monroe, Virginia.)

White southerners carry signs reading, "We intend to beat the Negro in the battle of life, and defeat means one thing— Extermination." Perceiving itself as the guardian of beleaguered black southerners, the North responded to "Black Codes" and other postwar abuse by supporting harsh military law for the South.

As the postwar months passed, northern demands for action in the South mounted steadily. The abolitionists, who had dedicated their lives to black emancipation, demanded that southern blacks be allowed to vote, and that the defeated South be punished. Republicans, who believed—correctly—that when southern blacks voted, they would vote for the party of Lincoln, also insisted on immediate black enfranchisement. That goal also received the backing of northern industrialists, many of whom had grown rich and powerful during the war. These titans now wanted to expand their businesses into the South, where they expected to find both a large pool of cheap labor and a vast new market for their products. Aware that the former slaveholding Democrats would, if they had the political backing, return the South to its old farming economy, the northern industrialists threw their support to the Republicans and others who wanted to crush the Old South and secure the rights of the freed blacks.

A popular 1865 cartoon shows Union officers guarding Confederate president Jefferson Davis. Although exaggerated, the picture reflected the facts: disguised in his wife's coat and shawl, the once icily dignified Davis was arrested by federal officials in May 1865 as he tried to escape through Georgia.

These powerful forces, along with a complex series of political maneuvers, resulted in the harsh era known as Reconstruction. In the midst of the war, two years before his assassination on April 14, 1865, President Abraham Lincoln had proposed a plan for the readmittance of the Confederate states. His program, along with that of his successor, President Andrew Johnson, was denounced as far too lenient by the Radical Republicans in Congress, who managed to impose their own plan within a year of the war's close. It consisted of a series of harsh Reconstruction Acts that established military law throughout the South,

Constitutional convention delegates assemble in Columbia, South Carolina. Expecting black delegates to be "barbarians," many white southerners admitted that they were impressed by the "remarkable moderation and dignity" of the "colored members."

intended to assure black rights, including the right to vote.

Under Reconstruction, the southern states' first job was to rewrite their constitutions, which would make possible their reentry into the Union. Delegates to the constitutional conventions were elected—under the watchful eye of the area's military commanders—by universal male suffrage, excluding only those whites who had been instrumental in the rebellion. (No American woman of any race would gain the right to vote until 1920.)

Now, with the Black Codes no longer enforced, African Americans went to the polls to help select delegates to the constitutional conventions. As a result, the delegate slates of each of the 11 former Confederate states included blacks. Their proportion varied from one state to the next; in South Carolina, for example, the majority of delegates was black, but in Texas, 81 of the 90 delegates were white. In most of the states, however, blacks were present in the conventions in about the same ratio as they were in the state population as a whole.

Impoverished and humiliated by their defeat, large numbers of southern whites had only mockery and curses for blacks' new political power. According to historian Smith,

> The bitterest denunciations of the southern press were reserved for its black delegates—"African savages," "gibbering, louse-eaten, devil worshiping barbarians," and the like. One [South Carolina] newspaper called the state's constitutional convention "the maddest, most unscrupulous and infamous revolution in history." The recently deposed governor of the state predicted "a war of races" which would be "the most terrific war of extermination that ever desolated the face of the earth in any age or country."

To the general surprise of the South, however, black and white delegates often managed not only to get along, but to earn each other's respect. The Charleston, South Carolina, *Daily News* had this to say about the state's convention delegates:

> Beyond all question, the best men in the convention are the colored members. Considering the influences under which they were called together, and their imperfect acquaintance with parliamentary law, they have displayed, for the most part, remarkable moderation and dignity. . . . They have assembled neither to pull wires like some, nor to make money like others; but to legislate for the welfare of the race to which they belong.

Black delegates also displayed generosity and a

Born a slave in 1841, Blanche K. Bruce had escaped, become an educator, entered politics, and earned a fortune as a Mississippi planter before being elected to the U.S. Senate in 1874. From the Senate, Bruce went on to a series of prestigious government positions in Washington, D.C.

spirit of conciliation. Beverly Nash, a delegate to the South Carolina convention, impressed his white colleagues with these words:

> I believe, my friends and fellow-citizens, we are not prepared for this suffrage. But we can learn. Give a man tools and let him commence to use them, and in time he will learn a trade. So it is with voting. We may not understand it at the start, but in time we shall learn to do our duty.

Nash was only one of the countless African Americans, many of them—like Nash himself—former slaves, who proved themselves outstanding leaders after the Civil War. Tall and good-looking, Nash started his life in freedom as a bootblack, then involved himself in politics, where he much impressed his colleagues, one of whom described him in these words:

> The lawyers and the white chivalry, as they call themselves, have learned to let him alone. They know more law and some other things than he does, but he studies them all up, and then comes down on them with a good story or anecdote, and you better believe he carries the audience right along with him. . . . No sir, there is now nobody who cares to attack Beverly Nash.

Nash clearly had the style that a good politician needs, but more than style, a black southern politician of his day needed courage. Many whites recognized the need to accept blacks in their previously all-white world; others were prepared to do anything to prevent it. It was men of this stripe who decided that former slave James Alston had no place in the Alabama legislature. One night soon after his election, Alston realized that a ring of men had surrounded his small house; in the next few minutes, 265 shots crashed through the still air. Shattering windows and walls, the bullets reached their primary target: two shells tore into Alston's body. The shooters fled, assuming their job was done, but they were wrong.

Alston recovered, only to receive a bald message:

pack up and leave town *now*. He said no. That night, the vigilantes returned, once again surrounding and shooting up Alston's little house. The gunmen managed to kill his horse and destroy his buggy, but Alston escaped. One of five black men elected to the Alabama constitutional convention, Alston appeared for the opening session. He was the only one; by then, his four colleagues had been shot dead.

In the long run, the mixed-race conventions produced a series of extremely progressive constitutions. They all abolished slavery, and many also eliminated property qualifications for voting and outlawed debtors' prisons. All the constitutions gave every adult male citizen, with the exception of certain Confederate leaders, the right to vote. Curiously, the strongest voices against the Confederate exclusions came from the black delegates. As Nash put it, "We recognize the southern white man as the true friend of the black man. . . . In these public affairs we must unite with our white fellow-citizens. They tell us that they have been disfranchised, yet we tell the North that we shall never let the halls of Congress be silent until we remove that disability."

During Reconstruction, which lasted until military rule ended in 1877, black voters put black representatives in the state legislatures. South Carolina, with 87 blacks and 40 whites in its lawmaking body, had the highest proportion, but the voters always elected white men as governors. Several states elected black lieutenant governors, treasurers, education superintendents, and secretaries of state. Southern blacks also represented their states in the U.S. Congress. Among them were a number of outstanding political leaders, including two Mississippi senators, Blanche K. Bruce and Hiram K. Revels.

Bruce won election to the U.S. Senate in 1874, making him the nation's second black senator (and the last until the 1966 election of Edward Brooke

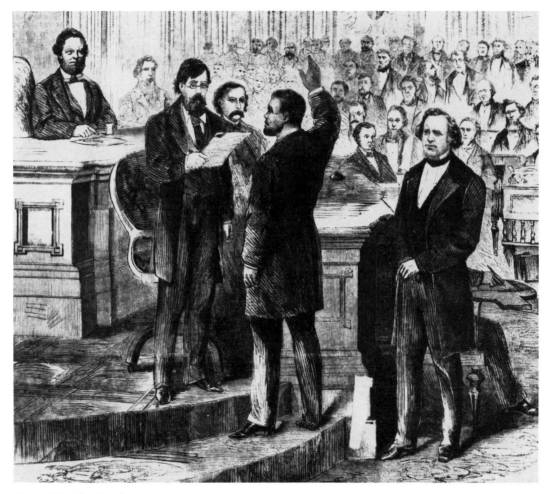

Hiram Rhoades Revels, the first African American ever elected to the U.S. Senate, takes the oath of office in 1870. Born free in 1822, Revels had been a clergyman before accepting the former seat of Jefferson Davis, the Mississippi senator who became president of the Confederacy.

from Massachusetts). Born a Virginia slave in 1841, Bruce escaped to Hannibal, Missouri, where he founded a black school. When the war ended, he studied in the North, then headed for Mississippi, entered politics, served as tax collector, sheriff, and county school superintendent, and eventually became a wealthy planter. After his term in the Senate, Bruce's talent secured him appointment as registrar of the U.S. Treasury. From 1889 to 1893, he served as recorder of deeds for the District of Columbia, and in 1895, he was reappointed Treasury registrar, holding the prestigious position until his death in 1898.

Hiram Revels was born free in North Carolina, raised in Ohio, educated at Knox College in Illinois, and later ordained a minister in the African Methodist Episcopal Church. When the war began, he joined the Union army, helped recruit other blacks, and served as a chaplain. Becoming active in Mississippi politics after the war, Revels not only had the distinction of being the first black U.S. senator in America's history, but of being the occupant of a rather special seat in the Senate: that of the onetime senator who became president of the Confederate States of America.

Contemporary white observer and wit George Templeton Strong found the irony of Revels's success irresistible. "O Jeff Davis, ain't this a go?" he chortled. "What do you think of the 'genman' who sits in your seat and represents your own . . . state? To this have all your intriguings and blusterings and proclamations and conscriptions come at last!"

6

MOVING FORWARD

BY the time the Civil War ended, most blacks, along with their white friends and supporters, had lost interest in the so-called Colonizationist movement, at one time seriously considered as a solution to the "Negro problem." Colonizationists had proposed that, once freed, all blacks should move out of the United States and set up their own nation. Bizarre as it may sound today, the Colonizationist movement found approval from well-intentioned people of both races, from Frederick Douglass to Abraham Lincoln.

Colonizationists endorsed a variety of sites for the new black homeland—Africa, Central America, Haiti, Europe, the unsettled American West—anywhere, as long as it was not white America. Some Colonizationists favored compulsory emigration; they would deport the blacks whether they wanted to go or not. Others, such as Lincoln, recoiled from

Bound for Liberia, Africa, a group of Arkansas blacks wait for their ship in New York City. Colonizationism, a scheme to resettle all America's blacks in Africa or other far-off places, gained wide popularity for a time, but by the early 1870s it had lost its appeal.

Packed to the rafters, the First African Baptist Church of Richmond, Virginia, resounds with rolling oratory from the pulpit. Christianity had long been important to African Americans, but after emancipation it became, notes one historian, their "most basic reality."

such an approach. Blacks' "emigration must be voluntary," he insisted, "and without expense to themselves."

Hoping for a consensus on the question, Lincoln called a group of northern black leaders for an August 1862 White House meeting. "Your race is suffering, in my judgment, the greatest wrong inflicted on any people," he told them. "The aspiration of men is to enjoy equality with the best when free, but on this continent, not a single man of your race is made the equal to a single man of ours." He went on to say that few white Americans believed that blacks and whites could live together on an equal basis. "Your race suffer very greatly, many of them, by living among us, while ours suffer from your presence," he said. "It is better for us both, therefore," he concluded, "to be separated."

Lincoln's arguments pleased some blacks, but they enraged others, and mail began to bombard the White House. A New Jersey man asked these blistering questions: "Pray tell us, is our right to a home in this country less than your own, Mr. Lincoln? . . . Are you an American? So are we. Are you a patriot? So are we. Would you spurn all absurd, meddlesome, impudent propositions for your colonization in a foreign country? So do we." A man from Philadelphia shared the New Jerseyan's views. "This is our country as much as it is yours," he informed Lincoln, "and we will not leave it."

"Why this desire to get rid of us?" snapped the editor of a black periodical, the *Anglo-African*. "Can it be possible that because the nation has robbed us for nearly two and a half centuries, and finding that she can do it no longer and preserve her character among nations, now, out of hatred, wishes to banish, because she cannot continue to rob us?"

Other blacks disagreed vehemently. The same publication, the *Anglo-African*, carried a plea for emigration:

> Listen—We want our rights. No one is going to *give* them to us, so perforce we must take them. In order to do this, we must have a strong nationality somewhere—respected, feared. . . . We can make of Haiti the nucleus of a power that shall be to the black . . . the hope of progress and the guarantee of permanent civilization. . . . From that centre let the fire of freedom radiate until it shall enkindle, in the whole of that vast area, the sacred flame of Liberty upon the altar of every black man's heart, and you effect at once the abolition of slavery and the regeneration of our race.

The Colonization movement finally died, has-
tened to its end by Lincoln's withdrawal of support
and by the emphatic opposition of Frederick Douglass.
Arguably the most eminent, most respected, most
influential black man of his era, Douglass was born a
Maryland slave in 1817. He illegally educated himself
and, at the age of 21, escaped to the North. Soon the
nation's leading abolitionist, he published a newspaper and numerous books and pamphlets, and lectured
to huge crowds all over America and England.

Like Lincoln, Douglass had originally favored a
black exodus from the United States, but by the time
the war started, he was implacably opposed to the
scheme. He and the rest of the nation's blacks, he
wrote, were "Americans, speaking the same language,
adopting the same customs, holding the same general
opinions, . . . and shall rise and fall with Americans."
Enlarging on his theme, Douglass wrote, "The hope of
the world is in Human Brotherhood; in the union of
mankind, not in exclusive nationalities."

The last word on black emigration came from
Richard Cain, elected to the U.S. House of Representatives by the voters of South Carolina in 1873.
When a white congressman urged a revival of the
Colonization movement, Cain took the floor. Speaking in the rolling tones of a seasoned orator—Cain
had long served as a clergyman (and later as a bishop)
in the African Methodist Episcopal (AME) Church—
the North Carolina representative held his colleagues
spellbound with these words:

> The gentleman wishes that we go to Africa or to the West
> Indies or somewhere else. I want to enunciate this doctrine
> upon this floor: we are not going away. We are going to stay
> here and work out the problem. We believe that God
> Almighty has made of one blood all the nations upon the
> face of the earth. We believe we are made just like white
> men are. . . . I am clothed with humanity like you. . . . Sir,
> we are part and parcel of this nation, which has done more
> than any other on earth to illustrate the great idea that all

races of men may dwell together in harmony. We will take that time-honored flag which has been borne through the heat of a thousand battles. Under its folds Anglo-Saxon and Afro-American can together work out a common destiny, until universal liberty, as announced by this nation, shall be known throughout the world.

Rather than head for the border when the war ended, many freed slaves took to the road in search of their families. As the "property" of others, slaves had sometimes been sold or traded with little regard for their family units. The reestablishment of these relationships was a spiritual triumph for their members that equaled or even exceeded emancipation. Helping to reunite splintered families were the Freedmen's Bureau and a large number of other agencies, especially the black churches.

African American churches had experienced an explosive increase after the war. Especially appealing to the poor and uneducated majority, black Christianity became "the most basic reality of the freed slaves," notes historian Page Smith. Black churches were not only places of worship but providers of education, mediators of disputes, sources of pride, centers of community social activities, and powerful political forces—which, a century later, would become the foundation of the great civil rights movement. The African Methodist Episcopal and Negro Baptist churches were the largest and most influential denominations, their combined membership reaching about 700,000 by the end of the Reconstruction era.

Before the war, many slaveholders had encouraged religious practices among their bondspeople, but theirs was a religion specifically tailored for the plantation. As one former Mississippi slave put it, "Ole missus used to read de good book to us . . . on Sunday evenings, but she mostly read dem places where it says, 'Servants, obey your masters.'" Now that she and her people were free, said the black woman, "Dar's heaps of things in dat ole book we is just sufferin' to learn."

Northern missionaries, both white and black, often wrote of the intense love and respect that the Bible inspired in freedmen. Men and women who had never been taught to read constantly asked these clergymen to share the "Good Book" with them. The Reverend David Macrae, a Scottish missionary stationed on a Texas plantation, reported that his black community owned two Bibles, cherished but inaccessible to the older residents. Every day, he wrote, "a little crowd" of young people who had learned to read came to his school "with messages from the parents and grand-parents at home, begging for the loan of one of their Bibles for the night, that they might have it read to them by their children." Deeply impressed by the attitude of his flock, Macrae wrote:

> Nowhere in America does one find such simple and child-like faith, such a strong belief in the presence and power of God, such fervor and religious enthusiasm, as among pious Negroes. They seem to see God bending over them like the sky, to feel His presence on them and around them, like the storm and the sunshine.

The one area in which the churches could provide little assistance was economic. Most former slaves stayed in the South after the war, and most wound up working for white landowners who persisted in treating their black laborers much as they had treated their black slaves. Some blacks migrated to the North, but the only jobs available, even for the well-educated, were those of laborers or service people: waiters, cooks, maids, and porters.

Blacks who looked for work in the expanding northern industrial base ran into problems at once. Wealthy factory owners played blacks against whites, often firing white workers who threatened to strike and replacing them with blacks. With no alternative in sight, the blacks were forced to accept the low pay and often miserable working conditions offered by the owners. Some black workers were unionized (either as members of all-black or integrated locals), but most were not, and the black unions found themselves opposed not only by the employers but by the white unions.

Stokers face searing heat as they tend the boilers of a northern foundry. Because black workers were rarely unionized— and were therefore forced to accept lower pay and wretched labor conditions—employers often sought them out for the toughest tasks.

In 1869, the National Negro Labor Union was formed, but the organization was unable to secure

Pioneering New Jersey businessman J. N. Vandervall used his own likeness in an advertisement for his East Orange carpet-cleaning factory. Like countless other black 19th-century entrepreneurs in the North, Vandervall designed his operation to appeal to the small but growing black middle class.

much for its members. If employers wanted to hire unionized workers, they could accomplish that end through the traditional, white-dominated unions. The greatest advantage in hiring black workers, many employers believed, was their lack of a strong labor organization. They could be hired for the lowest wages, would work in the most grueling areas of employment, and could be terminated at will by the

employer. The very availability of black workers provided employers with an effective bargaining tool
when negotiating wages and conditions with white
workers' unions.

The most prosperous black Americans were the
entrepreneurs, bright and ambitious men and women
determined to make their mark in the postwar world.
Mostly, they served the needs of their own communi-
ties, taking advantage of the segregation that kept
their customers away from white-owned businesses
and services. A separate black America began to de-
velop, with its own stores, cafés, hotels, taverns, thea-
ters, barbershops, laundries, livery stables, carpenters,
painters, doctors, and musicians. Self-employment
became a respected way of providing necessary services to other blacks, at the same time ensuring
financial prosperity, or at least stability, for the entre-
preneur's family.

7

BACKLASH

*All persons born or naturalized in the United States, and subject
to the jurisdiction thereof, are citizens of the United States and of
the State wherein they reside. No State shall make or enforce any
law which shall abridge the privileges or immunities of citizens of
the United States; nor shall any State deprive any person of life,
liberty, or property without due process of law; nor deny to any
person within its jurisdiction the equal protection of the laws.*

THE language of the Constitution's Fourteenth
Amendment is very clear: it guarantees the
rights of citizenship to all Americans. But, southern
legislators and lawyers were quick to point out, no-
where in its language did it *specifically* grant all citizens
voting rights. Anyone who had listened to the long
debate that preceded the amendment's passage, or
who had any knowledge of the day's political scene,
would have known that guaranteeing African Americans the right to vote had been among Congress's
highest priorities. Indeed, the congressmen who approved the Fourteenth Amendment never doubted
that it would secure the vote for all American blacks
and establish their equal footing as citizens.

*Southern blacks cast their ballots during Reconstruction.
The Constitution's Fourteenth Amendment, ratified in 1868,
appeared to guarantee blacks the vote, but not until passage
of the Fifteenth Amendment in 1870 were federal and state
governments specifically forbidden to deny the vote "on account
of race, color, or previous condition of servitude."*

African Americans pay homage to the "Great Emancipator." The Republicans had little trouble in securing the loyalty of black voters, who connected their freedom with the party of the Emancipation Proclamation and its author.

There was, in fact, much more than altruism at work when the Fourteenth Amendment was being pushed through Congress. Members of the Republican-dominated coalition that controlled Congress knew their days might be numbered after the defeated states of the Confederacy were readmitted to the Union. When that happened, southern whites would be able to exact revenge upon the Republicans by sending rafts of Democratic representatives and senators to Washington. The only way to counteract that reaction would be to sign up several million black voters in the South, who could help save a few dozen congressional seats.

The war had not even ended when Republican-controlled civic organizations—most prominently, the Union League of America—began enlisting black members in the South. This political proselytizing was magnificently effective for the Republicans, who offered black voters the choice of the "Great Emancipator's" party (theirs) or the party of slavery (the Democrats). Within a few years after the war's end, the Republicans had the southern black vote locked up almost entirely, and largely, though less so, in the North. Southern blacks would remain overwhelmingly Republican until the 20th century, when the Democratic party would become the stronger advocate of civil rights.

Former Confederates made every attempt imaginable to keep blacks from voting. Some of their methods were clearly illegal; they included threats, assaults, murder, and arson carried out by the Ku Klux Klan and similar organizations. Other more devious strategies were disguised in a veneer of legality; these included literacy tests, poll taxes (fees charged for voting), residency requirements, or simply the outright prohibition of voting rights for blacks.

Andrew Johnson stood no chance of election to the presidency in 1868, and General Ulysses S. Grant, whose military victories had helped Lincoln win reelection, defeated him easily. Grant had been in office less than two months when Congress approved the Fifteenth Amendment to the Constitution. Its language left no

A desperate African American batters vainly on a now-locked door. With the closing of the Freedmen's Bureau in 1872, blacks lost one of their major defenses against southern racism.

doubt as to its meaning, stating simply: "The right of citizens of the United States to vote shall not be denied or abridged by the United States or by any State on account of race, color, or previous condition of servitude. The Congress shall have power to enforce this article by appropriate legislation." The Fifteenth Amendment did not outlaw literacy tests or poll taxes that

were applied without regard to race. Those
mechanisms, as well as other bars to voting,
would remain in place until well into the
20th century, when Supreme Court decisions
and civil rights legislation outlawed them. The
amendment, however, was largely effective in
removing the states' arguably lawful barriers to
voting; illegal means of intimidation, though,
would continue to be used against potential black
voters for another century.

The Fifteenth Amendment was ratified in
March 1870, and within two years almost all the
former Confederates who had been deprived of the
right to vote or hold office had been restored to full
citizenship. All but a few hundred diehard leaders
of the rebellion were now free to take part in the
political process. Despite their oaths of loyalty to
the Union, they reentered the political fray with
their old values and agendas still in force.

By 1876, white Democrats controlled most of the
South. Grant was reelected by a huge margin in 1872,
although his administration was already marred by
substantial charges of corruption. As the people of the
North tried to put the Civil War behind them and
focus on their own economic development, the Republican party gradually began to transform itself from
one guided by idealists and dominated by abolitionists to one controlled by the wealthy and supported by
the upper classes of white native-born Americans. In
the North, the Democrats found support among the
working classes, Catholics, and immigrants. It was
inevitable that American blacks would eventually
become allied with the Democratic party, but this
alliance developed decades earlier in the North than
it did in the South.

Holding a "Republican ticket," a black would-be voter meets stony resistance from the White Leaguers who command the polls. The 1870s cartoon was not much overdrawn: the South actually had such a league, and its members did threaten, injure, and even kill blacks who showed an inclination to vote.

By the early 1870s, the Democratic forces that controlled the South had embarked on an ingenious and malicious lawmaking campaign, its goal the returning of blacks to their previous stations of inequality and powerlessness. They passed all manner of racist and unconstitutional laws, knowing full well that such statutes were by then unlawful. They knew it would take years to strike down such laws, as the challenges to them made their slow way through the federal court system. These laws, passed after the ratification of the

Fourteenth and Fifteenth amendments, were less bla-
tant in their terms than the Black Codes of the immediate postwar era, but their intents and effects were
identical.

The campaign of terrorism against blacks
continued as well, with several major objectives.
Foremost was a desire to keep blacks from voting
and thus gaining political power in proportion to
their numbers; this was accomplished through
organized intimidation and violent attacks that
increased in number as election days approached.
This approach was most effective in rural areas,
far removed from federal supervision. A second
objective was economic: blacks were now com-
peting with whites for jobs, especially those that
required no special skills. Blacks were willing to
work harder for less money, and even in the
South, many employers preferred black workers
for those reasons. By this point, blacks were not
the only victims of the Ku Klux Klan and similar
groups; the terrorists vented their rage on whites
as well, especially those who would employ black
workers or assist them in voting and political
organizing.

The group that suffered the most was the
black middle class, those who had been born into
freedom in the South and who had prospered
there for generations. Many whites who had been
wealthy before the war were now bankrupt; men
who had governed plantations were forced, for
the first time in their lives, to seek employment.
There was a massive upheaval of the social classes,
both black and white, in the South after the Civil
War. In fact, the prewar class structure had been

for most purposes destroyed. The semblance of courtesy that white southerners had shown toward free blacks before the war was replaced by hostility, and the black middle class disappeared along with the slaveholding aristocracy.

With President Andrew Johnson out of the way, the Republicans in Congress no longer had to worry about presidential vetoes; Ulysses Grant would go along with any reasonable request. But the Republican party itself was in the process of changing, and the country as a whole had tired of the Reconstruction era. There was a sense in Congress that the time for reconciliation had come. Congress had already enfranchised most of the former Confederates, including many who were responsible for the worst atrocities against the black soldiers of the Union army, along with Union prisoners of war of both races. With Grant in the White House, Congress could act with a simple majority, rather than depending on the two-thirds vote it had needed to override Johnson's vetoes.

Hoping to counter the repressive laws being passed in the South, Congress enacted the Civil Rights Act of 1875. It was a courageous and progressive piece of legislation, designed to accomplish some form of integration between the races, not only in the defeated Confederacy but in the North as well. Promptly signed by Grant, the law prohibited discrimination in public accommodations such as restaurants, hotels, and barbershops, and mandated that blacks be treated equally with whites in regard to jury duty. The act gave the federal government greater powers in eradicating discrimination, but its effect on day-to-day life in the South was nearly invisible.

Much of Reconstruction had ended by 1876, and the peculiarities of that year's presidential election accelerated the withdrawal of the last Union army troops still occupying the defeated Confederacy. The Democratic candidate, Samuel J. Tilden, received 250,000 more votes than his Republican opponent, Rutherford B. Hayes. But the election results from three southern states—Florida, Louisiana, and South Carolina—as well as those from Oregon, were disputed. This threatened to cause a crisis in Congress, because the election was so close that it was impossible to determine the victor without first evaluating the disputed vote. Anxious to avoid anything that might hamper the process of national reconciliation, Congress worked out an agreement.

Although Hayes had received fewer votes, a joint declaration of Congress declared him the winner, but this agreement was only reached when coupled with two promises. First, President Hayes would withdraw the remaining occupation forces as quickly as possible; second, Congress would open its coffers and spend freely on public-works projects in the South.

The promises were kept, and the last of the federal troops withdrew in 1877. Six years later, the Supreme Court invalidated the Civil Rights Act of 1875, declaring it unconstitutional. Almost three-quarters of a century would elapse before the Congress of the United States would again attempt to implement such a bold social reform.

8

IN PURSUIT OF FREEDOM

✳

DURING the Civil War and Reconstruction, black men built a solid record of achievements, many of them widely recounted. Equally impressive were the accomplishments of another minority group: black women. Some of their stories are well known: that of the courageous abolitionist and feminist, former slave Sojourner Truth, for example, has been admiringly told and retold from one generation to the next. Truth dedicated the last years of her life to the task of helping her fellows find meaningful employment—no small task in a society that usually limited opportunities for blacks to the lowest-paid and most strenuous forms of manual labor.

Harriet Tubman, the fearless abolitionist and Underground Railroad conductor who time and again risked her life to rescue black men and women from Maryland, site of her own former bondage, has acquired the status of mythic hero. "I never lost a

Underground Railroad conductor Harriet Tubman (far left) stands with a group of former slaves she rescued. Tiny, soft-spoken, and unable to read or write, Tubman nevertheless feared no one: if a man faltered on the terrifying road to freedom, she might put a gun to his temple, her lips to his ear, and rasp, "Move or die!"

Freeborn in 1825, Frances Ellen Watkins Harper must have been one of the 19th century's busiest women: an internationally recognized journalist, best-selling novelist, and extraordinarily popular poet, she was also a working member of the Underground Railroad, a temperance-movement leader, innovative educator, hard-traveling lecturer, women's-rights activist, and wife and mother.

passenger and I never ran my train off the track," proudly stated the woman known as the "Black Moses." And Tubman continued her humanitarian works after the war. No longer needed to free blacks from slavery, she tackled the daunting task of helping to free them from hunger and homelessness in a harsh postwar world.

Frances Ellen Harper is perhaps less familiar to today's reader, but she was the most popular black poet of her time; her *Poems on Miscellaneous Subjects,* which appeared in 1857, sold an astonishing 10,000 copies. Also the century's most prolific black novelist, Harper wrote several best-selling works of fiction, including *Sowing and Reaping: A Temperance Story* (1876) and *Iola Leroy* (1892). Born to free parents in 1825, Harper, whose best-loved poems ("The Slave Mother," "The Slave Auction") exposed the tragedy of human bondage, taught school in her native Baltimore, where she also became an active force in the abolitionist movement. Determined to improve not only her own race but all humankind, the idealistic Harper gave lectures on many subjects, especially temperance, to audiences across the eastern seaboard. As well as being a poet, novelist, public speaker, and reformer, Harper was a dedicated feminist, a friend and colleague of such women's-movement pioneers as Susan B. Anthony and Elizabeth Cady Stanton.

North America's first black female publisher, editor, and investigative reporter, Mary Ann Shadd Cary, was also the first black female lawyer in the United States. Born in Delaware in 1823, Cary moved with her family to Canada after the U.S. Congress passed the infamous Fugitive Slave Law of 1850. She was a cofounder of the *Provincial Freeman,* a newspaper designed for blacks in Canada, and the founder of one of America's first racially integrated schools. Returning to the United States in 1863, Cary became a recruiter—the only female of either race to be so designated—for the Union army, for which she also helped mobilize a black regiment. After the war, Cary opened a school for black children in Washington, D.C., where she also studied law at Howard University, receiving her degree in 1870. Ten years later, she organized the Colored Women's Progressive Franchise Association, a group designed to train black women to take responsibility for their own political and economic affairs. An ardent feminist, Cary tirelessly campaigned for equal rights for women of both races.

The list of black women who made their mark between 1863 and 1875 is a long one. Along with abolitionists Truth and Tubman and author-crusaders Harper and Cary, the catalogue includes Rebecca Lee Crumpler, who in 1864 became the first black American woman to earn a formal medical degree. A specialist in diseases that affected women and children, in 1883 Crumpler published *A Book of Medical Discourses*, advice for women on obtaining medical care.

Also on the achievers' list is Fanny Jackson Coppin, who became America's second black female college graduate when she earned her degree from Oberlin College in 1865. (Preceding her was another Oberlin graduate, Mary Jane Patterson, who received her B.A. degree from Oberlin in 1862.) In 1869, Coppin was named principal of Philadelphia's Institute for Colored Youth, making her the first black woman to head an American institution of higher learning. Charlotte E. Ray, another female achiever of the period, was admitted to the bar in Washington, D.C., in 1872, and became the first female African American lawyer allowed to practice law in any U.S. jurisdiction. (To avoid gender discrimination, Ray always signed herself "C.E." instead of "Charlotte.")

The post–Civil War period also saw black Americans making impressive strides in the fields of science and technology. Adding luster to their achievements

Sharp-tongued Mary Ann Shadd Cary (1823–1893) flayed opponents with such "unladylike" words as "moral monster" and "unclean bird," meanwhile preaching abolitionism, the need for women's rights, black independence, and economic self-reliance. An educator, newspaper publisher, editor, investigative reporter, and Union army recruiter, Cary was also the nation's first black female lawyer.

is the fact that few were highly educated or trained. Most, on the contrary, were workingmen who developed new technologies and processes through practical application and natural ingenuity.

One such inventor was Jan Matzeliger, a black Dutch Guianian who arrived in Philadelphia in the early 1870s and became an apprentice shoemaker. (Surprisingly, hundreds of black men and women immigrated to the United States during and immediately after the Civil War.) Matzeliger spent countless hours at his last, a foot-shaped form used in the manufacturing and repairing of shoes. Shoemaking had always been done by hand, but Matzeliger believed he could find a way to do it faster and more cheaply. Finally, he perfected the device he had dreamed of. Patented in 1883, Matzeliger's Lasting Machine was, according to the patent description, the first device "capable of performing all the steps required to hold a shoe on its last, grip and pull the leather down around the heel, guide and drive the nails into place and then discharge the shoe from the machine." Matzeliger sold his patent to the United Shoe Machinery Company of Boston, simultaneously making a fortune and revolutionizing the footwear industry.

Among other outstanding black inventors of the day was Elijah McCoy. The son of escaped slaves, McCoy was born in Canada in 1844 and grew up in Michigan. Young McCoy, always fascinated by machinery, went to Scotland to study mechanical engineering. Unable to find a job in his field when he returned home, he took a job as a railroad fireman. In those days, the engine, which needed frequent oiling, had to be brought to a standstill before it was oiled—one of McCoy's duties. Figuring there had to be a more efficient way of dealing with the process, McCoy studied and thought, and in 1872, he came up with an automatic lubricator that would function while the

Inventor Granville T. Woods is best known for developing a telegraph system that allowed moving trains to communicate both with each other and with railroad stations. Born free in Ohio in 1856 and known as "the Black Edison," Woods also invented the electric "third rail" still used in urban subway lines.

machine was moving. McCoy's invention eventually became mandatory in a broad array of machinery. It became so essential, in fact, that manufacturers often asked, before buying a new piece of machinery, if it was "the real McCoy," an expression still used to indicate authenticity. McCoy was later granted 57 patents for various mechanical devices, including an ironing board and a lawn sprinkler.

Granville T. Woods, born free in Ohio in 1856, loved trains. Forced to leave school at the age of 10, he got a job on a railroad, and spent his spare time studying books about electricity. He worked his way up to a position as an engine driver for the Danville

Nat Love, also known as Deadwood Dick, was born a Tennessee slave in 1854 and headed west 15 years later. He spent the next quarter-century driving cattle, fighting Indians, battling tornadoes and mountain lions, and making such friends as Sheriff Bat Masterson and outlaws Jesse James and Billy the Kid. "I led an unusually adventurous life," he once conceded.

and Southern Railroad, where he realized that many train accidents could be avoided if messages could be sent from one moving train to another and from a train to a railroad station. He finally invented and patented a telegraph system that would accomplish his aim, and later devised a system that enabled electric trains to draw their power from an overhead electric line. Earning the nickname "the black Edison," Woods went on to invent more than 60 train-associated devices, including the "third rail" now widely used by subways.

Although most blacks who left the South headed for the industrial cities of the northeast and Great Lakes states, a substantial number of former slaves and freeborn blacks went west in search of adventure and fortune. (By 1890, more than 500,000 black men, women, and children lived in Texas and Oklahoma alone.) In the West, blacks involved themselves in the same occupations that attracted their white counterparts: frontiersman, cowboy, horse trader, homesteader, fur trapper, prospector, and lawman—as well as gunslinger and desperado.

In his 1987 history, *The Black West*, William Loren Katz notes:

> Among the cowboys of the last frontier, 5,000 black men helped drive cattle up the Chisholm Trail [a cattle route that ran from San Antonio, Texas, to Abilene, Kansas] after the Civil War. The typical trail crew of eight usually included two black cowboys. Some had come west as slaves and were roping and branding cattle before they became free men. Others had come west after emancipation, seeking a new and free life where skill would count more than skin color. Some came to live by the law, and others rode in to break it.

One of the latter was Ben Hodges, half black and half Mexican, who blew into Dodge City, Kansas, in the early 1870s. Charming, good-looking, and silver-tongued, Hodges managed to swindle residents and

1

A PROMISE OF FREEDOM

✳

FOUGHT from 1861 to 1865, the Civil War marks the only period in which the United States was threatened with extinction. That savage and astonishing conflict, which pitted state against state, citizen against citizen, and brother against brother, has always fascinated Americans. Because it ended generations of slavery, it holds special resonance for black Americans.

By 1860, enslaved black men and women had toiled for white Americans for almost 250 years. Of the South's 9 million people, some 4 million were slaves, workers upon whom the area based its entire agricultural economy. Vehemently opposed to this state of affairs were millions of abolitionists, most but not all of them northerners, who considered slavery the deepest sin a society could commit, and who dedicated themselves to its abolition.

In 1860, the voters of the United States elected Republican Abraham Lincoln as their 16th president.

Americans of all races and ages celebrate the end of slavery in Washington, D.C. The embattled South ignored President Abraham Lincoln's 1863 Emancipation Proclamation, but the policy turned the Union armies into a force for black liberation.

13

Confederate guns pound Fort Sumter, the federal bastion off Charleston, South Carolina, on April 12, 1861. The fort surrendered on April 14, and by April 17 the nation was at war against itself.

Because his party firmly opposed the expansion of American slavery, it alarmed southern leaders, who feared that a Lincoln administration would sharply discriminate against their slaveholding population. These leaders had threatened that their states would secede (withdraw) from the Union in the event of a Lincoln victory. When it came to pass, that is exactly what they did.

First came South Carolina, one of the nation's 33 states; on December 20, 1860, it voted to secede. A month later, Mississippi, Florida, Georgia, Alabama, and Louisiana followed suit. On February 4, 1861, the Confederate States of America declared its nation-

Ben Hodges, remembered in Dodge City as "a notorious cattle thief and confidence man," strolls through the Kansas cowtown with a long rifle. The weapon was largely for show: Hodges was a crack shot but he preferred making his dishonest living by his wits.

visitors in Dodge City for more than half a century. In one of his more ingenious schemes, he portrayed himself as the heir to a vast Spanish land estate. Although he never proved his claim, he managed to use it in a number of successful schemes to cheat local bankers and merchants out of sizable sums of money. The residents of Hodges's adopted hometown, Dodge City, included a broad cross-section of native-born whites, blacks, Mexicans, European immigrants, and Native Americans, all of them accustomed to the town's ongoing swirl of gunplay and general violence. Hodges knew how to handle firearms, but he disdained gunplay. Instead, he lived by his wits. At one point, charged—probably justly—with rustling a herd of cattle, he transfixed—and amused—the tough cowtown's courtroom with a two-hour defense speech that included these words:

> What me, the descendant of old grandees of Spain, the owner of a land grant embracing millions of acres, the owner of gold mines and villages and towns situated on that grant of which I am sole owner, to steal a miserable, miserly lot of old cows? Why, the idea is absurd. No, gentlemen, I think too much of the race of men from which I sprang, to disgrace their memory.

The jury acquitted him.

Ned Huddleston, who later called himself Isom Dart, was born a slave in Arkansas in 1849. During the Civil War, Huddleston found himself near the front lines, but not in a soldier's uniform. Still in servitude, he spent his days foraging for food and cooking meals for Confederate officers. After he was freed, Huddleston headed for Mexico, where he worked as a rodeo clown, then became a horse thief, settling in a lawless part of northwestern Colorado known as Brown's Park. Deciding to change his ways, Huddleston became a gold prospector, then a bronco buster.

Huddleston—or Dart, as he was more often known—was said to have few equals as a horseman. "I have seen all the great riders, but for all around skill as a cowman, Isom Dart was unexcelled," recalled one contemporary observer. "He could outride any of them." Dart's skills could have earned him a good living anywhere in the West, but he loved adventure, and he soon reverted to his old ways. He found nothing more exciting than stealing horses and cattle, usually in the company of a small band of men known as the Tip Gault gang. An unusually lucky man, Dart was the sole survivor of an ambush that killed the other members of his gang; he stayed alive, he later

A soldier of the 9th Cavalry "listens" as a Native American bridges the language gap with sign language. Like many observers, artist Frederic Remington, who drew this picture, noted that when blacks and Indians were not fighting each other, they enjoyed an easy camaraderie.

reported, by spending the night in the grave of one of his dead comrades. A few years later, Dart was arrested for stealing cattle. On his way to jail, the deputy who had seized him lost control of his wagon and crashed into a ravine, injuring himself badly. Lucky again, Dart escaped harm, but instead of making a getaway, he stayed and saved the deputy's life. The grateful lawman testified at Dart's trial, and the jury let him go.

Dashing outlaws, of course, made up only a tiny percentage of the black wave that flowed west after the Civil War. A large number of African American westerners were cowboys, and many others wore the uniform of the United States Army. In 1866, Congress authorized the organization of black regiments—commanded, of course, by white officers—to settle the

Troopers of the legendary 10th Cavalry take a break at a New Mexico campsite in the 1870s. Formed at Fort Leavenworth, Kansas, in 1866, the 10th patrolled Arizona, New Mexico, Oklahoma, and Kansas, battling Comanches, Sioux, and Apaches, and helping capture such celebrated fugitives as Geronimo and Billy the Kid.

"Indian problem" of the West. The result was the formation and dispatch of four black units, the 9th and 10th cavalries and the 24th and 25th infantries.

Congress had been willing to authorize these black regiments for two main reasons: the desire to reduce Native American hostility against settlers in the West, and the splendid performance of black troops in the Civil War. "It is ironic," comments Katz, "that these brave black soldiers served so well in the final and successful effort to crush America's Indians, the first victims of white racism in this continent. But serve they did, following the orders of their government."

Despite inequities similar to those they faced during the Civil War—inadequate food, dilapidated equipment, and aging horses, to name a few—the blacks who served in the cavalry and infantry units in the West earned a reputation for diligence and heroism. They saw action against Indians, outlaws, and even some white settlers who resented their uniformed presence on the frontier. Nevertheless, discipline among the black troops was generally superior to that in white units, which had a higher incidence of drunkenness and desertion. To men raised as slaves, the spartan life of a soldier was no hardship.

The Plains Indians nicknamed the black cavalrymen "Buffalo Soldiers," partly because of their short, curly hair and partly as a tribute: they respected these black enemies, and they respected the buffalo, the animal central to their lives and culture. (The name stuck: World War II's famed combat unit, the much-decorated 92nd Infantry Division, had grown out of the old 24th Infantry, and it was still known as the "Buffalo Division.") Observes Katz:

> The Buffalo Soldiers served their country during an age of mounting anti-Negro violence and hostility and, paradoxically, helped bring the white man's law and order to the frontier. They suppressed civil disorders, chased Indians who left the reservation out of frustration or in search of food, arrested rustlers, guarded stagecoaches, built roads, and protected survey parties.

The 9th and 10th cavalries covered themselves with glory in the decades following the Civil War. Almost no report about them exists in which their valor, endurance, and devotion to duty are not praised highly. General John J. Pershing, a famed military hero known as "Black Jack" because of his association with the regiment, wrote, "It is an honor I am proud to claim, to have been . . . a member of that intrepid organization of the army which has always added glory to the military history of America—the 10th Cavalry."

But another officer of the 10th found no glory with the unit. Henry Ossian Flipper, the son of Georgia slaves, was the first black to complete training at the U.S. Military Academy at West Point. Taunted and

Lieutenant Henry Ossian Flipper, born to Georgia slave parents in 1856, became the first African American to graduate (in 1877) from the U.S. Military Academy at West Point. Heartbroken by his subsequent dismissal from the army on a trumped-up charge, Flipper nevertheless carved out an extremely successful civilian career as an engineer. He died in 1940; 36 years later, the army issued him an honorable discharge.

abused for four years by his white classmates—"I have been very lonely indeed," he wrote in a letter home, "and these fellows appear to be trying their utmost to run me off"—the black cadet stood it for the sake of the one thing in the world he wanted: a career in the United States 10th Cavalry. In 1877, he graduated 50th in a class of 76, and received orders to report to the 10th.

But a few years later, the young lieutenant was seen horseback riding with a white woman. Whether that ride triggered the next event is not known, but shortly after it, Flipper suddenly found himself court-martialed for "conduct unbecoming an officer and a gentleman." He was found guilty and dismissed from the service.

Versatile and highly intelligent, Henry Flipper had also studied civil engineering at Atlanta University. After he was forced to leave the army, he was swamped with job offers from both the public and private sectors. A shining success in civilian life, sought after for his diplomatic skills as well as his engineering expertise, he nevertheless spent the rest of his life trying—and failing—to clear his name with his beloved United States Army. Henry Flipper died at the age of 84 in 1940. In 1976, the army reversed its verdict, and gave him an honorable discharge.

In some ways, the story of this dedicated young military man parallels the story of his people at this time. Seven years old when Lincoln issued the Emancipation Proclamation in 1863, Flipper grew up in a South reeling between two worlds. The Civil War's end broke the chains that had kept 4 million people from freedom for more than two centuries. But legal liberty by no means erased the shadow of slavery and prejudice or the lack of education and training from which African Americans suffered. Not even courage and intelligence could defeat the massive wall of fear and distrust erected by white society against its new black counterpart.

Like numberless other blacks, Henry Flipper bat-
tled fiercly for his place in the sun; like those of
countless others, his efforts met with overwhelming
opposition. But he refused to surrender; although he
fell short of his main goal, he did succeed in making
a life in many ways triumphant. Lieutenant Flipper
never knew that his untiring quest for justice was
finally rewarded, but his determined refusal to accept
the smashing of his dream—like the determination
of thousands of other hopeful, ambitious men and
women of color—eventually breached the seemingly
impregnable wall that barred blacks from equality.

The years between 1863 and 1875 presented African Americans with a tumultuous series of profound
shocks. From freedom to renewed persecution in the
era of the Black Laws, from the promise of Reconstruction to the resurgence of terrorism, perhaps no era
presented more stunning contrasts. During these years
of hope and hopes deferred, America's blacks pressed
on, determined that the nation's promise, articulated
in the words of the Declaration of Independence—
"that all men are created equal"—would one day be
fulfilled.

FURTHER READING

✳

Bennett, Lerone, Jr. *Before the Mayflower: A History of Black America 1619–1964*. Baltimore: Penguin Books, 1984.

Du Bois, W. E. B. *Black Reconstruction in America*. New York: Atheneum, 1979.

Foner, Eric. *Reconstruction: America's Unfinished Revolution*. New York: Harper & Row, 1988.

Franklin, John Hope, and Alfred A. Moss. *From Slavery to Freedom*. New York: McGraw-Hill, 1988.

Hine, Darline Clark, ed. *Black Women in America: An Historical Encyclopedia*. Vol. 1. Brooklyn: Carlson, 1993.

Katz, William Loren. *The Black West*. Seattle: Open Hand, 1987.

Kunhardt, Philip B., Jr., et al. *Lincoln*. New York: Knopf, 1992.

McKitrick, Eric L. *Andrew Johnson and Reconstruction*. New York: Oxford University Press, 1960.

McPherson, James M. *Battle Cry of Freedom: The Civil War Era*. New York: Ballantine Books, 1988.

Redkey, Edwin S. *A Grand Army of Black Men*. Cambridge: Cambridge University Press, 1992.

Smith, Page. *Trial by Fire: A People's History of the Civil War and Reconstruction*. New York: Penguin Books, 1990.

Taylor, M. W. *Harriet Tubman*. New York: Chelsea House, 1991.

Washington, Booker T. *Up from Slavery*. New York: Gramercy Books, 1993.

Wikramanayake, Marina. *A World in Shadow: The Free Black in Antebellum South Carolina*. Columbia, SC: University of South Carolina Press, 1973.

INDEX

PICTURE CREDITS

CHRISTOPHER HENRY, a New York attorney who specializes in American immigration law, is the author of the Chelsea House biographies of civil rights leader Julian Bond, U.S. senator Ben Nighthorse Campbell, and Housing and Urban Development Secretary Henry Cisneros. Henry has also written biographies of Chief Justice William H. Rehnquist and Associate Justice Ruth Bader Ginsburg for the Chelsea House series THE JUSTICES OF THE U.S. SUPREME COURT.

CLAYBORNE CARSON, senior consulting editor of the MILESTONES IN BLACK AMERICAN HISTORY series, is a professor of history at Stanford University. His first book, *In Struggle: SNCC and the Black Awakening of the 1960s* (1981), won the Frederick Jackson Turner Prize of the Organization of American Historians. He is the director of the Martin Luther King, Jr., Papers Project, which will publish 12 volumes of King's writings.

DARLENE CLARK HINE, senior consulting editor of the MILESTONES IN BLACK AMERICAN HISTORY series, is the John A. Hannah Professor of American History at Michigan State University. She is the author of numerous books and articles on black women's history. Her most recent work is the two-volume *Black Women in America: An Historical Encyclopedia* (1993).